IF THOSE
BRICKS
COULD TALK

A COLLABORATIVE BOOK & FILM DEDICATED TO THE LAFITTE PUBLIC HOUSING DEVELOPMENT, 1941–2005

Lafitte Public Housing is where I came from. This is me. This is my history. This is my beginning.
—**Michelle Nelson**

I don't know what's so special, but I really love the people around that area. Right now, young and old, they're ready to take care of me. —**Harvey Reed**

Back then, we would play and your mama would say, "All right, walk them home." You always had somebody to walk with you. It was a great pleasure to sit underneath the grown-ups and listen to them talk about old times. All the courtyards were green with beautiful flowers. They even had contests for the best-kept yard. I remember the shoeshine man. I remember listening to the radio. Crochet curtains in the windows. Cookouts, the gumbo, the pies and cakes. —**Paulette Clay**

I was at 609 North Roman until Katrina. The best time was sitting out there with my neighbor, Ms. Virginia. We sat on the porch watching the circus–the squirrels running across the wires, young girls talking and clowning, the young boys on the corner doing the doo-wop. It was family. —**Emelda Paul**

Hey Ms. D

Abibblybop

You sure look sweet

Abibblybop, abibblybop

—**Double Dutch song from children in the Lafitte**

Despite the buildings being closed, there was still a little porch-sitting in the Lafitte during the first Mardi Gras back after Hurricane Katrina. Photograph by Rachel Breunlin.

Introduction

In 2006, less than a year after Hurricane Katrina, the Department of Housing and Urban Development (HUD), the Housing Authority of New Orleans (HANO), and the City of New Orleans formed a coalition to transform public housing. Four of the largest developments—C.J. Peete (formerly the Magnolia), B.W. Cooper (formerly the Calliope), the Lafitte, and St. Bernard—were slated for demolition. Most people around New Orleans were aware that a major form of affordable housing in the city had not reopened after the storm, but many, including those who lived in public housing, were not aware of the federally mandated review process that was supposed to open a public discussion about what the next steps would be.

Since the Housing Act of 1937, the federal government has created policies and financed programs that dramatically redesigned cities around the United States. In the name of affordable housing, but also "slum clearance," "urban renewal," and interstate highway construction, federal programs funded the demolition of many historic neighborhoods. In the 1960s, urban activists like Jane Jacobs began to speak out against the wide-scale demolition and to articulate what cultural memories and resources could be lost. This era of urban development was also at the height of the Civil Rights Movement. Activists concerned about racial justice argued that "slum removal" often displaced people of color from important home places that had helped buffer them against painful years of entrenched segregation.

The National Historic Preservation Act of 1966 was a response to the pushback against these policies. It created the National Register of Historic Places, a repository for buildings around the United States that were significant to American culture. The Register is maintained by the National Park Service in the Department of the Interior. Citizens can nominate buildings that they deem important, and if they

Steps in the Lafitte.
Photograph courtesy
of Dianne Cousin.

are listed on the Register, the buildings receive some level of federal protection from redevelopment and demolition. The Act also created an independent agency, the Advisory Council on Historic Preservation, so that if the federal government is involved in a project that will impact buildings that are on the Register, or have the potential to qualify, there will be a review process to try to avoid demolition, or, at the very least, "mitigate" the impact of tearing down those historic structures.

The dynamics between government and the many communities and cultures that fall under its purview can be complicated and contradictory. In the United States, some branches of the federal government, like the Department of the Interior, have been charged with protecting places that are historically or culturally important to our country, and other departments have implemented policies and projects that have damaged or demolished historic sites and buildings important to national and local histories.

The "Section 106" review process, named after where it is defined in the National Historic Preservation Act, attempts to bring different branches of the government together with concerned citizens to work on solutions. Section 106 "encourages," rather than mandates, protection of sites that are listed on or are eligible for the National Register. Some historic preservationists who have been through the process many times have sadly noted that sometimes it seems like a process of "document and destroy."

Despite the historic resources we have lost, documenting the lives of people who are displaced when neighborhoods are torn down is still an important process. For instance, Dr. Mindy Fullilove, a psychiatrist exploring relationships between our environments and health, has researched how being forced to leave one's home causes a feeling of "root shock." When a culture that has been nurtured through a number of generations is disrupted, Fullilove found that it causes a "traumatic stress reaction to the loss of some or all of one's emotional ecosystem." Being able to stay connected to the people in one's ecosystem, and to continue to share important historical and cultural ties, is crucial for displaced communities.

If Those Bricks Could Talk is a result of the Section 106 mitigation of the Lafitte Public Housing Development in the Fifth Ward of New Orleans. Located between Orleans Avenue and Lafitte Street, in the late 1930s, an integrated 19th-century neighborhood was torn down to build a segregated public housing for "colored" families. At the time, there was no attempt to document what the old neighborhood had been like. When the Lafitte was torn down after Katrina, the Section 106 process provided an opportunity. Of course, looking at the history of multiple displacements in the neighborhood, one may evoke an old Louisiana Creole proverb, *Chatte brilé di feu* [A burnt cat dreads the fire], but creating a more equitable future means knowing what's gone before.

As we have investigated the neighborhood before and after it was the Lafitte, we found that the racial categories of residents have changed throughout its history. In early census data, we see people classified by whether they were free or enslaved. There were other categories of distinction that no longer exist in census forms, such as "mulatto" and "colored." Today, federal documentation uses the term "African-American," while many people speak of themselves as "black." These changes demonstrate how race itself is a social construct rather than a biological reality. As this public history project shows, racism and segregation were also continually challenged in the neighborhood.

ACKNOWLEDGEMENTS

To create *If Those Bricks Could Talk*, the documentary team of Cornerstones, the Neighborhood Story Project, and Spyboy Productions filmed 16 in-depth life histories, hosted community mapping and photo collecting sessions at the Sojourner Truth Neighborhood Center, and did in-depth archival research on the history of the neighborhood. We also worked with Earch Search, Inc. to incorporate their archaeological and census data that was also a part of the Section 106 mitigation.

Lafitte oral history participants. **Top Row:** Emelda Paul, O.J. Jiles, James Andrews, Michelle Nelson, Parreletta Carter, Bruce Davenport, Mary Johnson, and Tapica Sparkman. **Bottom Row:** Joe Cayou, Paulette Clay, Lumar LeBlanc, Dwayne Brumfield, Diana LeBlanc, Dianne Cousin, Joyce Giles, and Harvey Reed, Jr.

Throughout the research process, we were guided by an advisory board that consisted of representatives from the former Lafitte and the Faubourg Lafitte housing communities, Enterprise Community Partners, Providence Community Housing, and the Louisiana State Historic Preservation Office. HUD and HANO were the federal and local parties responsible for carrying out the Lafitte Section 106 process. In addition, we'd like to thank the Amistad Research Center; Archives d'Outre-Mer de France; The Historic New Orleans Collection; the Hogan Jazz Archive; the Louisiana State Museum; Dale N. Atkins, Clerk of Civil District Court, Parish of Orleans, New Orleans Notarial Archive; the New Orleans Public Library's City Archives; and the Southeastern Architectural Archive for sharing images for the project. We'd also like to acknowledge a wonderful group of archivists, scholars, artists, and community activists who shared their own experiences, research, and art: Bruce Sunpie Barnes, Bruce Brice, Ron Chisom, Luisa Dantas, Bruce Davenport, Walter Gallas, Ryan Gray, Daniel Hammer, Christopher Harter, Scott Heath, Dayna Bowker Lee, Marion Longwood and her daughter Furtis, Mary Moore, Matt Morrin, Nicole Hobson Morris, Ashley Nelson, Michelle Nelson, Ed Newman, Jacques Morial, Emelda Paul, Katy Reckdahl, Sally Reeves, Helen A. Regis, Keli Rylance, Becky Smith, Tapica Sparkman, Joe Torregano, Michel Varisco, and Laura Westbrook.

We would like to give a special thank you for all the years of love Wayne Everard and Irene Wainwright put into the City Archives. Y'all continue to be an inspiration. To Gareth Breunlin for his beautiful graphic design; Abram Himelstein, G.K. Darby, and the staff at the Center for the Book at the University of New Orleans for their publishing expertise; and Siobhán McKiernan for copy editing.

And most importantly, we would like to thank the residents—past and present—who contributed their oral histories, and whose stories shaped the film and book. We dedicate the project to y'all.

It is the intent of this contract that all masonry work be sound, straight, true, first-class and complete in every respect, and that the exterior walls be so constructed that dampness will not get into them. All work shall be laid plumb, level, and true.

Brick for the facing work shall be new, whole, sound, medium or hard common brick made from clay or shale, evenly burned, free from cracks and badly warped surfaces and other surface defects; they shall be of a material and manufacture which has proven satisfactory over a period of years. Two bricks when struck together shall emit a clear ringing sound.

    —*From* Specifications for the Construction of the Lafitte Avenue Housing Project, New Orleans, Louisiana. Project No. 1-5. Sol Rosenthal, Jack J.H. Kessels, and Ernest W. Jones, Architects. November 20, 1939

Bricks

Clockwise from top left: Mary Johnson with Santa at a Christmas tree lighting; Derrik Moore, Chelsea Ann, and Dominique Moore in front of Mary Johnson's apartment in the early 1990s; Emelda Paul's neighbor, Ms. Virginia, who sold frozen cups and cakes to kids; Norman Batiste (*sitting*) and a friend pose for Parreletta Carter during Mardi Gras; Andre Harris with her sisters; Dianne Cousin's son Marlon and his friend in front of his grandmother's apartment; Parreletta Carter's cousin, godson, and son-in-law near her front porch; Paulette Clay's mother Virley, Debbie, her sister Louversa, and daughter Caprice on Paulette's porch; Dianne Cousin's family; Bruce Davenport (*middle*) with his mother and grandmother inside their apartment; Emelda Paul's daughters Ava and Aura. *Center:* Looking out over Orleans Avenue in 2005. Photograph by Rachel Breunlin. *Opposite Page:* Brick masonry from a building in the Lafitte. Photograph by Bruce Sunpie Barnes.

Top left: An early photograph of Lafitte in the 1950s from HANO's archive. *Bottom left:* Emelda Paul's daughters Ava, Wanda, and Aura in their Sunday best, courtesy of the Paul family. *Right:* Parreletta Carter holding a brick from the Lafitte. Photograph by Bethany Rogers.

"She was a brick house, baby."

—Wanda Dubouse in *The Combination*

In the 1990s, the Lafitte Public Housing Development was 50 years old. Hitting the half-century mark, its 77 brick apartments could be designated as "historic" by the United States Department of the Interior. Ferdinand Bigard, who grew up on St. Ann Street in the Sixth Ward, had always admired the craftsmanship of the buildings. As Big Chief of the Cheyenne Hunters Mardi Gras Indian tribe, he had his own artwork on permanent display at the Smithsonian, and he knew of the importance of honoring work done by hand. Bigard put together an application to have the project listed in the National Park Service's National Register of Historic Places. In the application, he wrote about the brickmasons who built it. The buildings' physical presence was a blueprint of the masons' movement and balance. The individual bricks, small enough to hold in their hands, were carried and carefully lined up so they were plumb. Many of the men lived in the downtown neighborhoods of New Orleans, and proudly traced their trades back to family members who were free people of color. Their trade was part of their freedom. But like many New Orleanians, Bigard was also aware of how bricks have held contradictory meanings in the memory of the city. As part of his documentation, he also listed a brickyard in the area that contained housing for enslaved Africans who were forced to work there as early as the 1700s. At different times and places, bricks in New Orleans have held different meanings. They have meant confinement and also safekeeping. They have been sought after and shunned. Built up and torn down.

Above: An excerpt of "Veue et Perspective de la Nouvelle Orléans," a drawing by Jean Pierre Lassus in 1726, shows the early settlement of New Orleans between the Mississippi River and the *cypriera*, or cypress swamp. Image courtesy of Archives d'Outre-Mer de France. *Below:* Red brick dust, and a bottle of sulphur. Bottle courtesy of the New Orleans Pharmacy Museum. Photographs by Bruce Sunpie Barnes.

1 The first bricks in the city came from the red ochre clay made from the silt that floated down the Mississippi, spilled over the banks of the river during floods, and filled up the watery land around it. The brickyard that Ferdinand Bigard wrote about was located outside of the city on Bayou Road. It was created when the *Companie des Indies* [Company of the Indies] controlled Louisiana through a contract with the French Crown. Enslaved Africans dug out the clay from the swamps around them. Mixing it with sand, they poured the mixture into wooden molds and then fired them in a kiln. Using this method, they produced 50,000 bricks per month.

The red clay brick in New Orleans was not very strong because of its high concentration of sand. When it dried, it crumbled. Brick masons realized they needed to coat the bricks with stucco or a render of lime to give them extra support. With this technique, they built large parts of the city, as well as towers and walls around it. After the fires of 1788 and 1794, the Spanish were even more conscious of rebuilding with a material that had already gone through extreme heat to come into existence. Today, the "soft red" bricks are highly coveted by architects and contractors restoring old homes in the city.

2 Throughout the 19th and first half of the 20th century, the ease with which the bricks crumbled launched another business. Peddlers kept a steady trade selling red brick dust on the streets of downtown neighborhoods. Residents of the Lafitte/Tremé area would have participated in a longtime tradition of warding off any evil that might try to pass through the entrances of their homes. As the poet Brenda Marie Osbey's poem "Faubourg" recalls, it was part of women's housekeeping rituals:

yatta leaves must be dried and woven into belts and baskets
rags must be burned in sulphur to ward off mosquitoes
and slave brick crushed and scrubbed across doorways.

The practice turned the steps bright white. A certain alchemy occurred. The stolen labor it took to create many of the soft red bricks was broken down, resold, and turned into protection,

3 In New Orleans, brick masonry was a craft that could provide economic security if you could make it through the apprenticeship. Wilbert F. Monette's father was a bricklayer and cement finisher. Wilbert said his father started him out with a shovel:

Three days after, we sat down to eat lunch and I told him I didn't come out there to be a laborer. He told me, "You are going to learn this trade the way I want you to learn it. If you learn it out of the ground, you'll never have to worry about a job." From there, I carried for the bricklayers, mixed mortar, put material out for them, and then I grabbed a trowel and got in the line whenever I could. This is how I started laying bricks. Many times, he'd leave and when he'd come back, he'd tear it all down and say, "This isn't what I told you to do."

Bricklayers like Wilbert's father stood behind their work. It was a physical representation of their reputations, and they'd rather tear down a wall than jeopardize their names. Rudy Hutchinson grew up in the Seventh Ward among craftsmen as well. At night, he went to Booker T. Washington, a trade school that opened uptown in the Third Ward, to take advanced classes in blueprint reading, painting, and brick masonry. He recalled, "That's the only place blacks could go." It was a good time to learn a craft because of the millions of dollars in federal money coming into the city to fund the construction of public housing. Rudy remembered:

The plaster trade was hitting its boom during the time they was building the projects and all. The government had a lot of projects going, bringing work into play. I worked on the Lafitte Projects—they was all brick and plaster.

4 Across Lake Pontchartrain, the Schneider Brick and Tile Company was being celebrated in the leading trade journal, *Brick and Clay Record,* in 1937 for a clay found on the northshore of the lake. The journal reported it created lightweight bricks that could change into "a remarkable array of color" depending on the temperature that was used to make them. HANO contracted with the company to create bricks of different shades for each public housing development in the city. Unlike mass-produced bricks that are dyed to create a uniform color, these handmade bricks were what brick masons often called "honest" and full of slight variations. Lafitte's buildings had tones of orange and brown. They were trimmed with red wrought iron porches, balconies, and front doors. Wilbert F. Monette, who laid the bricks, explained:

A lot of people think it's easy. It's not easy. When you lay that first coat, you have to know where you are headed, what goes into that wall when you get to a certain height. If you're not right, then it will be a mess. If you are working under someone and all of it come down, you know you don't have no job no more.

Left: Building the Lafitte, from a HANO annual report in 1940, courtesy of the New Orleans Public Library's City Archives. *Middle:* Photograph of the Lafitte from the 1950s, courtesy of the HANO archive. *Right:* Tambourine and Fan parading past the Lafitte Projects in spring of 2005. Photograph by Rachel Breunlin.

The residents of Lafitte felt secure in the craftsmen's work, and neighbors outside of the development admired them. Shirley Simmons remembers, "I was envious of our friends who lived there; we lived in a wood house, they lived in a brick house." Anytime there was a storm coming, people from all around the city came to stay in the apartments. They knew the strong wind wouldn't rattle the buildings.

5 It wasn't just the weather. Throughout the second half of the 20th century, social upheaval around racial integration swirled around the Lafitte. A youth-based organization, Tambourine and Fan, was started in the neighborhood by civil rights workers Jerome Smith and Rudy Lombard. The group was concerned about the spirit of children growing up in an unstable society full of broken promises. The children of downtown New Orleans learned about other young people around the world who were separated from each other because they had different cultural, religious, or racial backgrounds. Every spring, they organized a parade called Super Sunday to raise awareness. The parade began on Bayou St. John and went down Orleans Avenue, past the Lafitte, to Hunter's Field on North Claiborne Avenue. Jerome explained:

We painted bricks yellow that we used in the day camp and brought with us to the bayou. Each brick was some country where children were suffering—the South African, the Palestinian, the Jewish, the Irish children—and behind the bricks we had a sign that said, "The tears of the child is a man's shame."

The children from the Lafitte and Tremé painted bricks a color of hope, and asked spectators and participants in the parade to value childhood as a way to build a new culture of social justice.

6 Up until Hurricane Katrina, nearly 2,000 residents, including almost 800 children, lived in the Lafitte. Despite Ferdinand Bigard's efforts, the community did not make it onto the National Register of Historic Places. The City of New Orleans' "Tremé Historic District" also did not include the Lafitte, and was thus not subject to the Historic Landmark District Commission's oversight. The hurricane brought 2 to 12 inches of water into some of the first-floor apartments, while others remained dry. There was no structural damage to the buildings. According to a survey of almost 400 Lafitte residents conducted by All Congregations Together, more than 90 percent of people who hadn't come back to the city wanted to return to New Orleans. Two residents who came back to see their apartments after the storm were Tapica Sparkman and Mary Johnson:

The Lafitte locked and empty after Hurricane Katrina. Photograph by Bethany Rogers.

Tapica: I didn't have water damage, but when I came back, I was like, "What is going on?" You couldn't get in.
Mary: HANO gave us a date and time, even if you were out of town, to come and pick up your stuff.
Tapica: Now I really know how a homeless person feels.

With iron security windows and doors on the buildings, the future of the Lafitte was uncertain. In 2007, the Louisiana Landmarks Society listed it on its "New Orleans' Nine" most endangered architectural sites. Jerome Smith shivered as he told investigative reporter Katy Reckdahl, "From the front to the back, there used to be kids there. It wasn't cold, but I got goose pimples thinking of the children and the absence of their sound there."

7 Although there was a compelling reason to open up public housing to support residents' right to return home, HANO's money for rebuilding was tied to federal dollars that stipulated the buildings be torn down and replaced. Explaining the decision to tear down the projects and build new housing, HUD spokeswoman Donna White said, "It's old and it would take millions of dollars to repair buildings that basically warehoused poor people." With dramatic cuts to federal funding of public housing and concerns about "concentrations of poverty," national housing policy had been moving toward creating private-public partnerships that were charged with tearing down old buildings. Unbeknownst to many residents, prior to Katrina, HANO had already begun to plan for the

Tearing down Lafitte. Photograph by Michel Varisco.

redevelopment of the Lafitte and other developments around the city. When the decision came through after the storm, there was a wide range of opinions from Lafitte residents, but most worried they wouldn't be able to return to New Orleans. The former president of the Lafitte Residential Council, Emelda Paul, explained:

People were very upset. We were under the impression we were coming right back. I said, "No, they're not going to take our project away from us. We're going to fight to the bitter end for this."

Local activism from residents, housing advocates, and urban planners like Bob Tannen compelled *The New York Times* architectural critic Nicolai Ouroussoff to write a piece addressing HUD's stereotypes of public housing developments in New Orleans:

[T]he low red-brick housing blocks of the Lafitte Avenue project...are scaled to fit within the surrounding neighborhood of Creole cottages and shotgun houses....As you move deeper into the complex, the buildings frame a series of communal courtyards sheltered by the canopies of enormous oak trees. Nature, here, was intended to foster spiritual as well as physical well being. That care was reflected in the quality of construction as well. Solidly built, the buildings' detailed brickwork, tile roofs and wrought-iron balustrades represent a level of craft more likely found on an Ivy League campus than in a contemporary public housing complex.

The rubble of the Lafitte. Photograph by Michel Varisco.

For many residents, the individual bricks, nestled together, came to symbolize the physical and emotional closeness people shared. When she heard the news that they would be torn down, Lafitte resident Paulette Clay said, "I cried and cried because each one of those bricks meant something." Lumar Allen, the leader of the Soul Rebels Brass Band, grew up in the Lafitte, and his tuba player, Damon, still lived there before the storm. When Damon told him they were starting to tear it down, Lumar thought:

"No, brah, those bricks could survive anything." One weekend I went back and was like, "Lord!" They had a trash pile the size of King Kong. I wanted to get a brick to keep as a memento. When I went back the next day, they had put fences all around it.

8 The Housing Authority of New Orleans contracted with Enterprise Community Partners, Providence Community Housing, and L+M Development to redevelop the project into "Faubourg Lafitte." *Faubourg* is a French word which translates as "false town" or "suburb," and was a common way of describing neighborhoods around the city during the French colonial period. Providence and

Constructing "Faubourg Lafitte." The new development is slated to have a "one-for-one" replacement of all 896 housing units that were in the Lafitte. Photograph by Harry Connolly, courtesy of Enterprise Community Partners.

Enterprise developed a community engagement process to collaborate with residents of the Lafitte on the redesign of the neighborhood. Working with All Congregations Together, a team of eight people, including former Lafitte residents, began to make thousands of phone calls to track down residents scattered in 37 different states. As they began to come back to New Orleans, they worked with Enterprise and Providence in planning workshops and design charrettes to help envision the new development. The new buildings are built with wood, and the clapboard houses were designed to blend into the Fifth and Sixth Wards' architecture. In total, 1,500 new units are planned in Faubourg Lafitte and the surrounding neighborhoods, including 100 homes for sale to families with "moderate" incomes.

9 In the film *If Those Bricks Could Talk*, Lafitte residents take us through their experiences in the neighborhood, sharing not just the development itself but the schools, churches, and small businesses of the area that were important to the community. A companion to the film, this book explores the broader history of the Fifth and Sixth Wards of New Orleans, and how the story of the Lafitte grew out of it. In researching this history, a dialogue between the hopes of the 19th and 20th centuries developed. We hope that the project shows how the goals of creating safe, affordable housing are deeply connected to struggles for racial justice. We offer the stories of river sand and clay from the banks of Lake Pontchartrain, brickyards on the edge of town, brick masons and dust peddlers, brick installations and keepsakes as offerings to both.

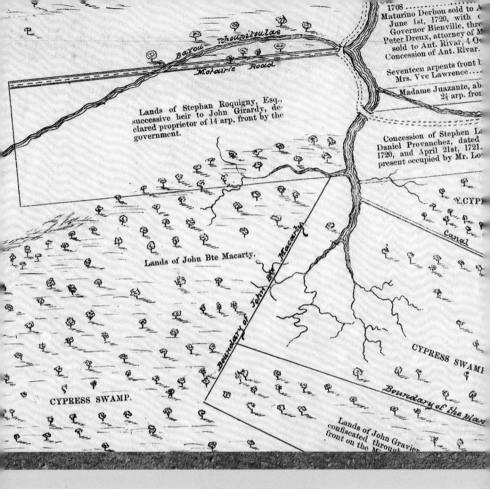

Bayou Tchoupitoulas

Metairie Road

Lands of Stephan Roquigny, Esq., successive heir to John Girardy, declared proprietor of 14 arp. front by the government.

1708 . . . .
Maturino Derbou sold to
June 1st, 1720, with
Governor Bienville, thre
Peter Dreux, attorney of M
sold to Ant. Rivar, 4 Q
Concession of Ant. Rivar.

Seventeen arpents front
Mrs. Vve Lawrence. . . . . .

Madame Juazante, ab
2½ arp. fro

Concession of Stephen L
Daniel Provanchez, dated
1720, and April 21st, 1721.
present occupied by Mr. Lo

Boundary of Jean Bte Macarty

Lands of John Bte Macarty.

CYPRESS

Canal

CYPRESS SWAMI

Boundary of the plan

CYPRESS SWAMP.

Lands of John Gravier
confiscated through
front on the M

An excerpt from "Plan of the City of New Orleans and the Adjacent Plantations compiled in accordance with an ordinance of the Illustrious Ministry and Royal Charter, 24 of December 1789, signed Carlos Trudeau" shows the Carondelet Canal running through cypress swamps toward the city from Bayou St. John. Further downtown, the land around Bayou Road has been sold to different property owners. As a navigable waterway, Bayou St. John was a passageway to the Gulf of Mexico through Lake Pontchartrain. Map courtesy of The Historic New Orleans Collection, Gift of Boyd Cruise and Harold Schilke.

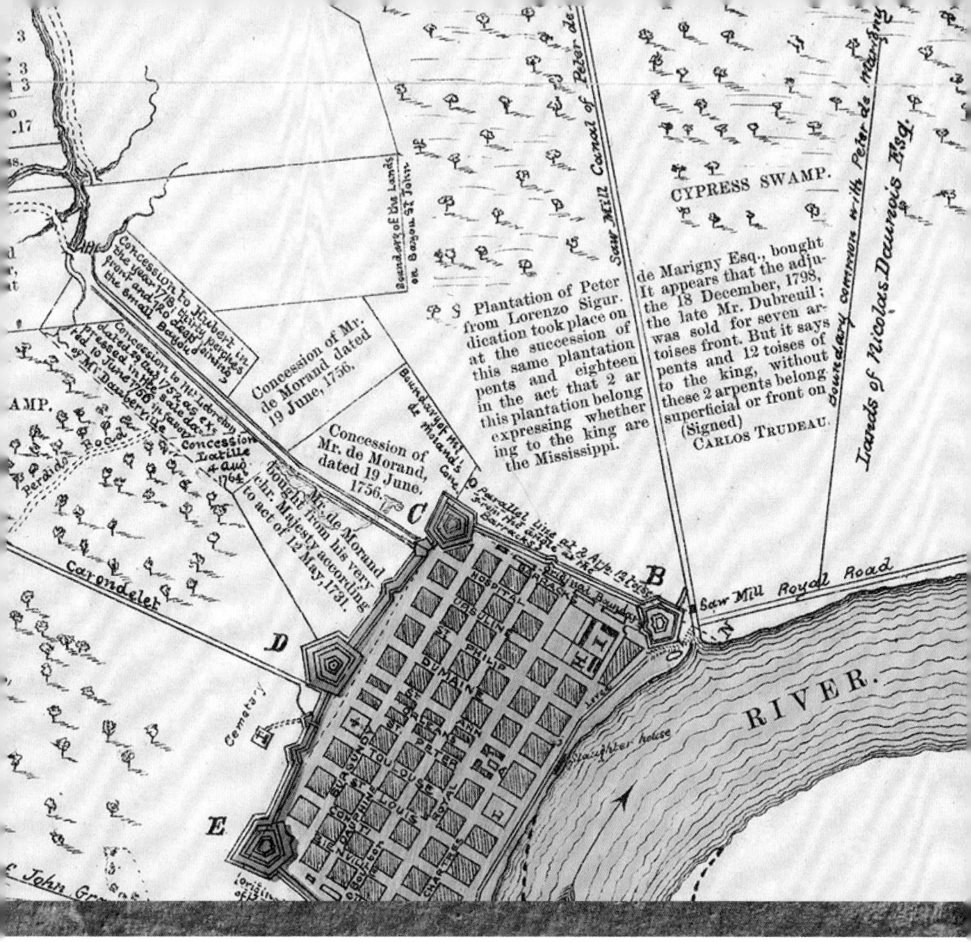
CYPRESS SWAMP.
Plantation of Peter
from Lorenzo Sigur.
dication took place on
at the succession of
this same plantation
pents and eighteen
in the act that 2 ar
this plantation belong
expressing whether
ing to the king are
the Mississippi.
de Marigny Esq., bought
It appears that the adju-
the 18 December, 1798,
the late Mr. Dubreuil;
was sold for seven ar-
toises front. But it says
pents and 12 toises of
to the king, without
these 2 arpents belong
superficial or front on
(Signed)
Carlos Trudeau.
Lands of Nicolas Daunois Esq.
Saw Mill Canal of Peter de
Concession of Mr. de Morand dated 19 June, 1756.
Concession of Mr. de Morand, dated 19 June, 1756.
Mr. de Morand bought from his very chr. Majesty according to act of 12 May, 1731.
Saw Mill Royal Road
Carondelet
Cemetary
Slaughter house
RIVER.
B
C
D
E
Hospital
Ursuline
St. Philip
Dumaine
St. Peter
Toulouse
St. Louis
Barracks

History of a "Back-a-Town" Neighborhood

There was a time when New Orleans faced the Mississippi River. As you moved away from its natural levee, you headed "back-a-town," where enormous cypress stands rose high above Creole cottages. Residents of the city considered the swampy land below sea level uninhabitable except for a sliver of high ground, the *Chemin du Bayou Saint Jean*—a remnant of an old tributary of the river.

This route in and out of the city, known to us now as Bayou Road, was an old Indian portage four miles long. It ran from Bayou St. John to the river. Local Choctaw tribes used the dry land as a trading ground, and early colonists, including free people of color, made new lives for themselves along the road. On the edge of the cypress swamps, the brickyard Ferdinand Bigard wrote about was built near their market gardens and sugarcane fields.

A postcard of the Carondelet Canal, circa 1910, courtesy of the New Orleans Public Library's City Archives. Not a very deep canal, in its heyday it was 30 feet wide. Boats used this waterway to bring in supplies from other parts of Louisiana that were then used to expand the city beyond the *Vieux Carre*. Lumber and cordwood from ancient cypress trees and yellow pine from north of Lake Pontchartrain traveled into the city and were milled in sawmills along the canal. Other vessels carried fish and oysters from the Tchefuncte and Tangipahoa rivers north of the lake. New Orleanians themselves could board small boats from the canal to travel to port cities along the Gulf Coast.

In the 1790s, Louisiana's Spanish governor, Francisco Luis Héctor de Carondelet, organized the excavation of a canal running from the bayou to right outside a fortress wall that ran along Rampart Street. It took two years to construct the waterway. It was built by convicts who had been held in the city's jail and enslaved people who were also forced into the project after the governor encouraged their owners to "donate" their labor. The economy of bondage made it possible for Carondelet to brag that the whole civic endeavor cost only 30 dollars. In his honor, the city named a promenade bordering the canal the "Carondelet Walk." Between this canal and Bayou Road, a mixed-use, multicultural neighborhood began to develop that would eventually include the Lafitte Public Housing Development.

EXPANDING AND DRAINING NEW ORLEANS

Located at the back of the city, the Carondelet Canal was largely ignored during its first few decades. In 1810, the *Louisiana Gazette* reported that it was "an unwholesome morass, from which pestilential emanations are continually evaporating." In other words, it had become a drain for the city's sewerage and smelled terrible. But there was reason why back-a-town deserved better.

By 1810, the city's original population had tripled. New Orleans was a predominantly black city, whose residents included 10,824 enslaved people, 5,727 free people of color, and only 8,000 whites. The combination of Americans moving to New Orleans from other parts of the country along with large waves of immigration from Ireland, Germany, and St. Domingue (Haiti) meant that the city had to expand beyond its original borders.

Downtown, the Creole-speaking community spread out from the French Quarter and Bayou Road into the Faubourgs Marigny and Tremé. The *terres vacantes*, or vacant land, around the Carondelet Canal became more valuable, and efforts were made to clear out and widen it. Irish immigrants who were desperate for work joined convicts and slaves who waded into the water to dig out the land by hand.

An excerpt of "Diagram Showing the Inundated District, Sauvé's Crevasse, May 3rd, 1849, Ludwig Von Reizenstein, ca. 1850," courtesy of The Historic New Orleans Collection. This map of New Orleans shows the way the city expanded throughout the 1800s and was divided into three municipalities after the Louisiana Purchase. In the 1830s, the New Basin Canal and the Pontchartrain Railroad, which ran along Elysian Fields, overtook the Carondelet Canal as the primary conduits linking the city with Lake Pontchartrain.

On May 3, 1849, the Mississippi River overflowed from a crevasse at Sauvé's plantation, and a large part of the city flooded. The Third Municipality, located downtown outside of the French Quarter, was spared because of the Carondelet Canal's levee. When citizens from other parts of town tried to break the levee to equalize the flooding, residents of the area armed themselves and took up guard.

By the eve of the Civil War, the population of New Orleans had greatly expanded, and power dynamics around race changed dramatically as the city's white population increased. In 1860, the census counted 149,063 whites, 10,939 free people of color, and 18,068 slaves. Harsher laws against people of color began to restrict their ability to travel and participate in the local economy.

Throughout the 19th century, the city flooded on a regular basis, and the different civic calls for a systematic drainage and sewerage system were received by the public with skepticism. The dredging of canals (rather than mosquitoes) had been mistakenly associated with outbreaks of infectious diseases like yellow fever, and residents were wary of being surrounded by more water. In the 1830s, however, the city dug drainage ditches from the French Quarter to Claiborne Avenue that connected to the Girod Canal on Orleans Avenue. A pumping station with a steam engine pulled the water in the canal into Bayou St. John. Now surrounded by two commercial waterways, the Tremé/Lafitte area, nestled between the Carondelet and Girod canals, became one of the most well-drained in the city. It was subdivided into lots for housing in the 1840s and became a little Venice on the edge of the city.

MIXING

During the Civil War, New Orleans came under Union control much sooner than other parts of the South. By 1862, the city was occupied by federal troops. During Reconstruction, the state's new constitution legislated equal rights for all. Hopes ran high for a new society committed to racial justice in both the law and day-to-day life.

In the old Creole suburbs, people of many different backgrounds were used to living close together. They shared space, but not the same civil rights. In census data from the late 1800s through the 1930s, residents of the Tremé/Lafitte area listed their heritage as French, German, Italian, Scottish, Irish, and Spanish. Many identified as "mulatto" or "black." Mixed families included a German man named Henry Mank who lived with his wife, Annie, a Chinese woman born in Cuba, and their children. Black families rented property from white ones, and vice versa. The census notes show how their collective work contributed to all parts of the city. They were plasterers, bricklayers, house painters, and blacksmiths. They worked on the water as captains of schooners, fishermen in Lake Pontchartrain, and longshoremen who did "river work." They were shoemakers and horseshoers, bicycle mechanics and switchmen for the railroads.

As midwives, they visited women's homes to deliver babies and as carriage drivers for undertakers, they picked up loved ones who had passed on. They were police captains, watchmen, teachers, and firemen. They were clerks, printers, and secretaries. They called themselves laundresses and washwomen, tailors and seamstresses. They made dresses and cleaned hats. They ran stalls at the French Market. They were butchers, bakers, and cigar makers. They shucked oysters at saloons and were porters at pharmacies.

Some may have done odd jobs, but very few were unemployed. Many of the residents of the area created institutions that supported the health and well-being of their community.

Top: "Plan de 2 Terrains au Faubourg Tremé," Voilquin, 16 April 1839. After the 1840s, the Tremé/Lafitte neighborhood developed into streets full of small shotgun doubles and four-room Creole cottages. Larger buildings built of brick and masonry were developed near the more prestigious areas along the two canals. Notarial records show how the housing fit into the landscape created by the two canals. *Bottom:* In "Plan of (Lots and Buildings, Second District," F.N Tourné, 21 March 1862, the neighborhood is called "Second District" in English rather than the French "Faubourg Tremé." Images courtesy Dale N. Atkins, Clerk of Civil District Court and Ex-Officio Recorder, Parish of Orleans, Notaria Archives Division; Plan Books 61, folio 53, and 44, folio 68, respectively.

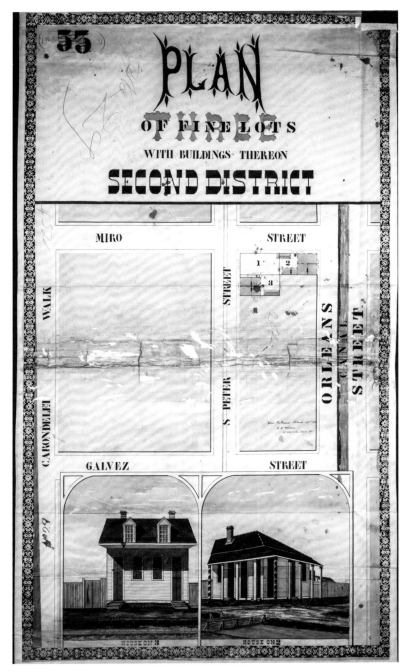

"Plan of Three Fine Lots with Buildings Thereon, Second District," by L.N. Olivier, 17 March 1868, gives a closer look at the Orleans Avenue Canal with a small wooden pedestrian bridge. Image courtesy of Dale N. Atkins, Clerk of Civil District Court and Ex-Officio Recorder, Parish of Orleans, Notarial Archives Division; Plan Book 38, folio 52.

Housing located in the area where the Lafitte was later built between North Prieur and North Johnson Streets, Orleans Avenue and St. Peter Street. The drawings come from "Plan of 8 Lots of Ground with Buildings Situated in the 2D District," A. Castaing and J.A. Celles, surveyors, undated, circa 1865-1866. Image courtesy Dale N. Atkins, Clerk of Civil District Court and Ex-Officio Recorder, Parish of Orleans, Notarial Archives Division; Plan Book 44, folio 17.

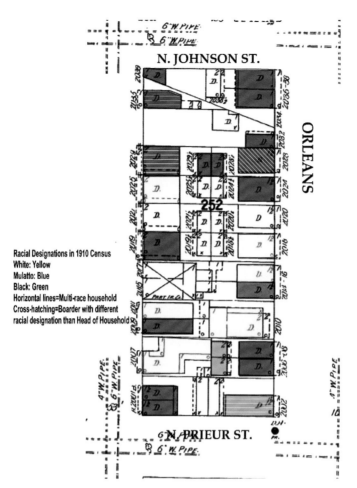

Racial Designations in 1910 Census
White: Yellow
Mulatto: Blue
Black: Green
Horizontal lines=Multi-race household
Cross-hatching=Boarder with different
racial designation than Head of Household

A map of the same block as left, created by Ryan Gray. Ryan and fellow archaeologists with Earth Search, Inc. worked on the Section 106 mitigation of Lafitte. Between the footprints of two buildings from the Lafitte projects, they uncovered the remains of a row of brick townhouses (facing St. Peter Street), frame cottages (fronting Orleans Avenue), and small "service" buildings that may have held a kitchen or servant and slave quarters during the antebellum era, but were converted to small apartments by the late 1890s. The collection of homes remained mostly unchanged until the 1930s.

Ryan's review of census data, correlated with street addresses, shows us who would have lived in these houses. It seems that the area was predominantly Creole, as most families identified as "mulatto" rather than "black" and carried French-derived surnames. However, many families lived in houses that also rented apartments to white families. There are also a number of multiracial households. In 1880, for instance, three heads of household were identified at 2019 St. Peter: Marie Mulct, a white 36-year-old widow from France (with her six children), while the other two, the Labostrie and Hill families, were designated as mulatto. Living with the Hills were Mrs. J.B. and Juanita Lopez, teachers identified in the census as white (and of Spanish and Italian parentage). Another example of a mixed residence came from the 1900 census, where an Irish widow named Mary Meade owned and resided at 2018 Orleans, along with a black barber named Joseph Daunois who also lived at the address with his wife, daughter, and niece.

It was not uncommon for some neighbors' racial designations on the census forms to change over time. For instance, a widowed mulatto seamstress in 1910, had, by 1920, become a white widow of French parentage. Anti-miscegenation laws often forced the census takers into contradictory conclusions. The race of individuals of Latin American or Caribbean descent commonly appears to be determined by the race of their spouses. In the hand-written manuscript census, items in the race column are frequently crossed out and changed.

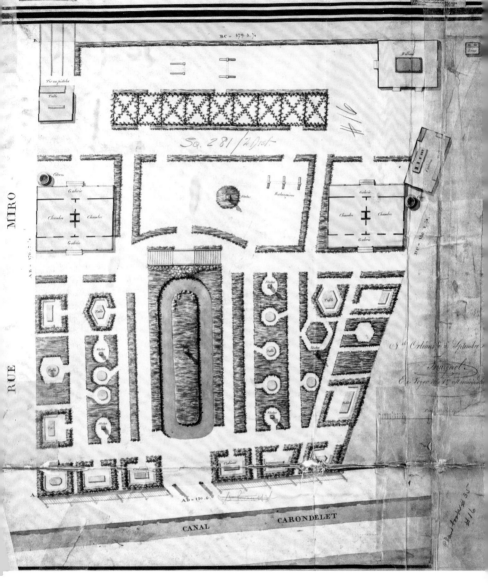

PLAN
DU JARDIN DU ROCHER DE Ste HÉLÈNE

Along the wide, tree-lined levee of the Carondelet Canal, there was a popular promenade where a number of private pleasure gardens were open to the public. The Jardin du Rocher de Ste. Hélène included a bar, pool tables, a pistol-shooting range, outdoor cookstoves, and swings. The garden had a formal European layout with statues and fountains, and a long bower—a wooded structure covered in plants and vines for shade. As the canal declined, however, the expensive upkeep of the gardens gave way to other uses for the land. By the late 1800s, the garden had been replaced by houses and storage buildings. Image comes from "Plan du Jardin du Rocher de Ste. Hélène," Jean Antoine Bourgerol, surveyor. September 5, 1844. Image courtesy of Dale N. Atkins, Clerk of Civil District Court and Ex-Officio Recorder, Parish of Orleans, Notarial Archives Division; Plan Book 35, folio 16.

Abolitionist and civil rights organizer Thomy Lafon was the son of a free woman of color from Haiti and a white French father. His philanthropy supported the free press *The Tribune*, and the Thomy Lafon Orphan Asylum in the Tremé/Lafitte area. When he died, he passed on his wealth to charities, "irrespective of race, color, sex or age." In 1896, the Catholic Sisters of Charity built a three-story brick building for the asylum at 1720 St. Peter between North Claiborne and Derbigny. Thirty-four orphaned "colored" boys ranging from four years old to 14 lived here with the nuns. On the next block, Louis Prima, the Sicilian musician and entertainer, grew up in a house at 1812 St. Peter. Both blocks were torn down to build the Lafitte. Photograph courtesy of old-new-orleans.com.

In 1861, the French Benevolent and Mutual Aid Society opened a hospital on the corner of Orleans and North Derbigny, which was in operation until 1947. The three-story building was sold to a national black Catholic fraternal organization, the Knights of St. Peter Claver, in 1951 for its headquarters. During the 1960s, the group rented offices to the National Association for the Advancement of Colored People (NAACP), as well as to civil rights attorneys such as A.P. Tureaud and Ernest "Dutch" Morial. In the 1980s, the fraternal organization decided the large building was too expensive to maintain and tore it down, despite protests. This photograph, courtesy of the New Orleans Public Library's City Archives Works Progress Administration Collection, shows what the area looked like after the Girod Canal was covered in the 1930s, but before the I-10 expressway was built in the 1960s.

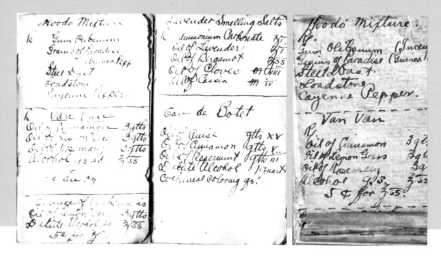

Recipe books for healing. Photographs by Bruce Sunpie Barnes from exhibits at the New Orleans Pharmacy Museum.

BLESSINGS AND TEACHINGS

By the late 1880s, Creole culture in downtown New Orleans felt the pressure of assimilating into the English-speaking majority. Lafcadio Hearn's writings, although leaning toward the nostalgic, give us a glimpse of how residents of the area were responding:

The later colored generation is proud of its correct French and its public-school English...[but] happily all the "colored Creoles" are not insensible to the charm of their maternal dialect, nor abashed when the invading Amerikain superciliously terms it "Gombo." There are mothers who still teach their children the songs—heirlooms of melody remnant with fetich words—threads of tune strung with grigris from the Ivory Coast. So likewise...are transmitted the secrets of that curious natural pharmacy in which colored nurses of Louisiana have manifested astounding skill—the secret of fragrant herb medicines which quench the fires of swamp fever...

Church was a place where language, spirituality, and healing were blended together. Looking through the census data of the Tremé/Lafitte area, we do not find any formal churches listed. We imagine that St. Ann's, the Catholic church on the other side of the Girod Canal, would have been the parish church for many residents of the area. The congregation was integrated, with services in Creole. Throughout the week, and at all hours of the day, parishioners regularly crossed the canal for blessings. Holy water, for spiritual well-being as well as protection against outbreaks of yellow fever, was in high demand.

During the same time, some of the public schools in downtown New Orleans were integrated. In 1868, the Bayou Road School admitted 28 girls whose families were *gens de couleur* [people of color]. Enrolling their children was a brave decision. When the school board found out, it reprimanded the principal, Mrs. S. Bigot. In her defense, she argued that she was unable to tell what the students' racial designation should be. The school board ordered her to find the students and remove them, but other reports indicate that the backlash against social equality may have subsided for a while. More than a decade later in 1877, the school board identified Bayou Road School as one of the last

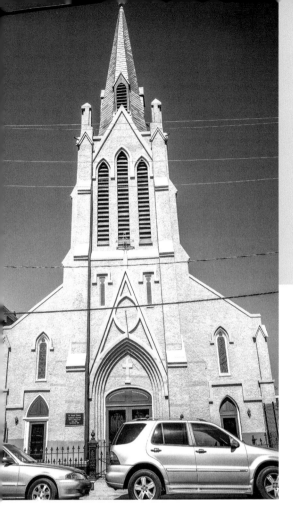

St. Peter Claver, formerly St. Ann's, on St. Philip and North Prieur in the Sixth Ward. At the turn of the century, a new priest at St. Ann forced services to be in English rather than Creole and told black parishioners to sit at the back of the church. In 1920, the parish split into two separate, segregated parishes with the original church becoming St. Peter Claver and the white parishioners relocating St. Ann's a few blocks away to Ursulines Street. The decision was part of a long series of battles over shared social, political, and religious institutions. Photograph by Bruce Sunpie Barnes.

schools in the city that was still integrated. Similarly, in Tremé/Lafitte, while half of the white parents pulled their children out of the Claiborne Boys' School when it was integrated, many returned over the course of the next few years.

In 1898, the new state constitution enacted laws that rolled back the goals of Reconstruction. In 1900, under the leadership of school board president E.B. Kruttschnitt—the nephew of U.S. senator Judah Benjamin and the leader of the Louisiana constitutional convention that eliminated equal rights—public education for "colored" students was reduced to the first five grades, and kindergarten was eliminated. The numbers speak for themselves: In 1910, the city had 16 colored public schools and 68 white ones. Until 1917 (when McDonogh 35 was established), there was no high school for colored students, and many of the battlegrounds for civil rights in the city became focused on elementary education.

The ongoing fate of Bayou Road School illuminates some of these struggles. After the brief period of integration, the school was designated as a colored school and given very few resources for upkeep. For over a decade, community leaders fought for a new school building, until the school board finally came through and built a new one on the same site in 1922.

The decision occurred just as the New Orleans City Council passed an ordinance that prohibited "Negroes from establishing residence in white neighborhoods and white residents from living in Negro districts." Over the course of the next five years, this law was challenged over and over again in the city, and it was eventually struck down in 1927 by the U.S. Supreme Court in *Tyler v. Harmon*. However,

LaBranche's Drug Store on North Claiborne, courtesy of the Charles L. Franck and Franck-Bertacci Photograph Collection at The Historic New Orleans Collection. The drugstore opened in 1905 and was known for its old-fashioned soda fountain. First used to make tonics for medicine, the fountains were used to make nonalcholic drinks during Prohibition. Many Lafitte residents remember being given a free drink from the soda fountain by Emile LaBranche with the proof of a good report card.

as historian Marcus Christian has written, in the years in between, "the ordinance had the effect of reviving racial animosities and encouraging racial ill will." This was certainly the case in the Sixth Ward, where white parents simultaneously argued that the new school for black children was too nice and that it was dragging down their property values. With the backing of self-proclaimed white supremacist and school board president James Fortier, they campaigned to have the building turned over to white students. The black community organized a response, and appointed a Creole pharmacist named Emile J. LaBranche as chairman.

LaBranche's family had been involved in opposing the development of Jim Crow laws after Reconstruction. Since 1905, they had owned a popular drugstore on North Claiborne Avenue. The boulevard was lined with two rows of live oak trees that canopied a wide neutral ground. A streetcar line ran beside it. The commercial corridor became known for its black-owned small businesses, as well as shops run

Left: The first Joseph A. Craig school replaced the old Bayou Road School in the Sixth Ward. The building eventually became Joseph S. Clark Senior High, the second public high school in New Orleans for black students. *Right:* Emile LaBranche working at the pharmacy. Photograph courtesy of the LaBranche Family Papers at the Amistad Research Center.

by Bengali peddlers from India and a Chinese laundry. Segregation based on skin color continued to be challenged. As historian Marcus Christian pointed out:

> *[P]ersons of colored races, such as Japanese, Chinese, American Indian, Puerto Rican, Filipinos, and South Americans all sit before the screen in the part of the vehicle reserved for whites. Dark whites, such as Turks, East Indians, and Spaniards, do likewise.*

Many streetcar drivers had the same difficulty as Principal Bigot in determining the "race" of their patrons. Marcus Christian studied a number of the discrimination cases brought to court in New Orleans in the years after *Plessy v. Ferguson*, quipping that the law burdened every street car driver with the "difficult task of [becoming a] competent anthropologist." In 1921, Mrs. Mary Glenn Cashman and Mrs. Jeanne Serpas Ruiz sat in the the "white-only" section of a streetcar on North Claiborne and refused to move after the conductor accused them of "being Negro." Like Rosa Parks years later, the women were arrested. In protest, they filed suit against the transit company, and won settlements of $250 and $100, respectively. These cases, long buried in civil rights histories, would have been important news in neighborhood businesses like LaBranche's at the time, and garnered more support for taking action against unequal education.

At a school board meeting, Emile LaBranche argued that colored children had attended the school for 40 years with overcrowded conditions. "Last year, the board again investigated, but this time they did build a new school, Joseph Craig. We now come to you and ask that you open to the colored children this school which has been built for them." The board eventually agreed to let the students temporarily move into the building until they built another school on St. Philip Street in Tremé, which opened in 1927.

Aerial shot of the Fifth and Sixth Wards shows the difference in layout between the Lafitte and the surrounding neighborhoods. The area that used to be the Carondelet Canal is in the foreground, and the North Claiborne neutral ground runs through the middle. As the city's drainage system and shipping technologies improved, neighborhoods expanded towards the lake, and the Carondelet Canal was filled in. The Southern Railway still ran along the side of it, and Lafitte Street was created between the train tracks and the Lafitte. The Girod Canal on Orleans Avenue, on the other side of the Lafitte, was filled in during the Works Progress Administration's public works program in the 1930s. Large Aerial Photograph #28, Set C from 1949 courtesy of the New Orleans Public Library's City Archives.

TEARING DOWN TREMÉ/LAFITTE FOR PUBLIC HOUSING

The same year Joseph A. Craig opened the city declared the Carondelet Canal unnavigable. While the Carondelet Canal had been in the shadow of the New Basin Canal for many years, construction of the Industrial Canal in the Ninth Ward made the sleepy old canal seem obsolete. For the next 50 years, this neighborhood that once linked the city with the rest of the region through waterways built by the Mississippi delta and the hard labor of the city's disenfranchised people, began to get cut off by other local and national policies as well.

No longer surrounded by water, the area was still bounded by wide streets and the Southern Railroad line. The Housing Act of 1937, however, dramatically changed its physical and social landscape. Offering long-term loans for first time home buyers, the federal act also designated money to build public housing. Although *Tyler v. Harmon* had declared residential segregation illegal, the policies implemented by both parts of the Housing Act encouraged racial discrimination and segregation. The Federal Housing Authority (FHA) refused to give loans in inner-city, multiracial neighborhoods like the Tremé/Lafitte. Loan applicants had to be white, and had to buy single-family "detached" homes in solely residential areas. Essentially, they had to move to the suburbs. Around the South, the federal government deferred to "local customs" and reinforced Jim Crow laws by building segregated public housing. In New Orleans, these new developments created social and physical distance between people in ways the city had never seen before.

It happened at a time when the city was growing again. Between 1929 and 1935, its population increased by 60,000 people. Although many black families around the South followed the Great Migration up North, many others moved into Southern cities like New Orleans. They arrived after leaving oppressive conditions of sharecropping and without much school experience. Many could only find accommodations in overcrowded housing. In the mid-1930s, 40 percent of all city residents lived in substandard housing. In HANO's annual report in 1937, the loan application to the United States Housing Authority was quoted:

Private enterprise has not kept pace with the growth of the community and from statistics accumulated and analyzed, relative to vacancies and the existence of unsatisfactory dwellings of low cost or rent, there is a demand for immediate construction of a large number of dwelling units of the low rental group.

Federal money for public housing could solve the housing shortage, but there were stipulations. The housing could not be built on vacant land because the funding was tied to "slum clearance." To qualify, New Orleans had to identify neighborhoods it considered "slums," and tear them down. The designation was subjective. It's true much of the 19th-century housing in New Orleans was ramshackled. Many families lived in old shotgun homes whose rooms ran one into the other, and still used outhouses in the backyard. However, the housing that was torn down was often in better shape than the housing that remained. For instance, the Tremé/Lafitte area had sewerage lines as early as the 1890s, and much of the housing in the area surveyed around the same time was considered to be in good condition. However, other considerations were also important. HANO's 1937 annual report explained that other criteria for the sites included being "accessible to transportation facilities. They must be near schools. They must afford reasonable recreational and community accommodations. The sites should have the advantage of clinical or hospital services." The Tremé/Lafitte neighborhood fit all of these requirements.

A collage of photographs showing properties slated to be torn down to build the Lafitte was published in a Housing Authority annual report from 1939. Image courtesy of the New Orleans Public Library's City Archives.

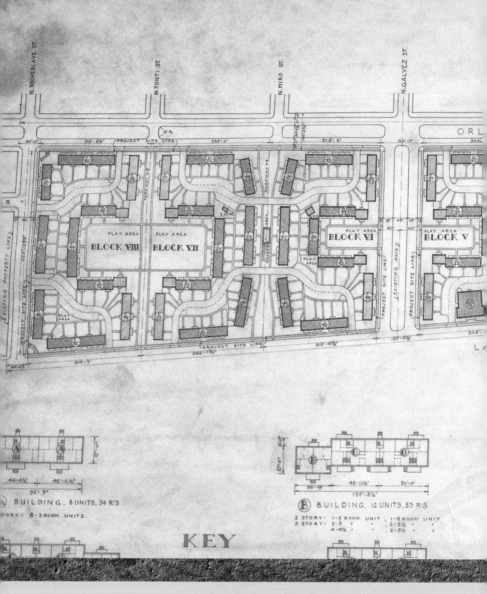

Details of the 1939 architectural drawings of the Lafitte Avenue Housing Project, No. LA 1-5, designed by Sol Rosenthal, Jack J.H. Kessels, and Ernest W. Jones, show the layout of the new development. Image courtesy of the Southeastern Architectural Archive at Tulane University. Architectural historians have argued that the design was inspired by the Pontalba Apartments on Jackson Square in the French Quarter.

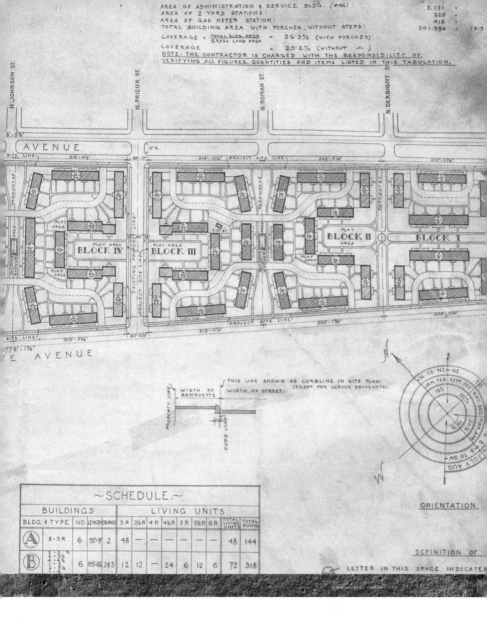

The Lafitte Years

An early photograph of the development shows young people playing horseshoes as part of programming with the New Orleans Recreational Department. Photograph courtesy of the New Orleans Public Library's City Archives.

MOVING OUT/MOVING IN

Public housing in New Orleans took integrated neighborhoods around the city and divided them into segregated developments. Uptown, a section of the Irish Channel was turned into the St. Thomas Public Housing Development for white families, and in Central City, the Magnolia was designated for "colored" families. Downtown, the area that had once been Storyville was torn down to build a white development called the Iberville, and the Tremé/Lafitte neighborhood was designated as "colored." Each development was named after a street that ran along its perimeter. HANO acquired the land in 1939 and the construction began in 1940. The first residents moved into the new development on June 4, 1941.

Where did all the people who lived in the Tremé/Lafitte go when the neighborhood was torn down? White residents were not eligible for the new development. Perhaps they were able to find apartments in the Iberville. We don't know if residents who identified as "black" or "mulatto" moved into the new development, or found new homes in other parts of the city. Little documentation exists. Newspaper articles in the black-owned *Louisiana Weekly* encouraged residents in other project areas, such as Central City, to move out of the condemned homes as quickly as possible. An editorial said that to qualify for the new public housing, families would have to show a "background of decency" and "good morals." The editorial also questioned the selection process by calling some of the interviewers hired by HANO "abusive." Reasons for not being eligible included poor housekeeping and "personal difficulties." One family who met the employment qualifications was rejected because the husband was "insolent" and had "too many suits." Clearly, deference to housing officials was required. A perceived excess of self-pride could jeopardize one's application. There are no reports of how a "racial screening" process was determined, but one can imagine that counselors were put in the same position as principals and streetcar drivers who were asked to enforce the laws of Jim Crow segregation—they had to guess.

From oral histories, we do know that many long-term residents of the Lafitte trace their family backgrounds to Mississippi, Arkansas, and rural Louisiana. Their families came to New Orleans in the first part of the 20th century looking to escape the rigid racial segregation of the post-plantation economy. Mr. Harvey Reed, Jr., for instance, was born in the delta town of Helena, Arkansas, in 1927 and moved into the Lafitte when he was a teenager. Other residents came from different neighborhoods in New Orleans, and the blend of city and country backgrounds made up the new community.

Parreletta Carter lived uptown on Delachaise before moving into the development around the same time as Harvey. She remembered:

They were just putting up the doors. My first apartment was at 646 North Galvez Street. My oldest girl, Charmaine, was born up in the court[yard]. After I had my baby, I moved to Johnson Street in a two-bedroom, and I had Terry. My oldest is 50 and my baby girl is in her 30s. We had two beautiful big live oak trees in the Johnson Court, and I had my big long porch. We used to have suppers, and you enjoyed yourself at night. In the driveway, they used to have people come out and show you how to play ball. They had a lady come and show you how to sew and crochet.

In its early days, part of the concept behind public housing was to provide social support services along with affordable housing. HANO offered courses on nutrition and cooking, developed programs for young people to go to the public library, hosted fashion shows, and supported groups for the "elderberries." It also employed "home counselors" who inspected residents' apartments to make sure they were clean and upholding the standards of "good housekeeping." While it was framed as support, it was also a reminder that one's home was not fully one's own. Some residents remember the visits as part of a law and order that they missed later on, while others felt it was an invasion of their privacy and made plans to move out of the development.

Many families raised three and four generations in the project. Michelle Nelson's grandmother, Ms. Liddie, came from Mississippi and raised her family in the French Quarter until the Desire Public Housing Development opened. Michelle said, "We stayed there all the way up to Hurricane Betsy in 1965. After Hurricane Betsy, we moved up into the Lafitte." Michelle was raised by both his grandmother and his mother. He raised his own children in the Lafitte.

Left: Elderberries Oldsters' Club sponsored by the YWCA. *Top right:* A "home counselor" visit. Photographs from the HANO annual report in 1961. *Bottom right:* Marion LeBlanc, one of the first residents to move into the Lafitte, in 2004, courtesy of the LeBlance family.

May 12, 1980

Life stages in Lafitte: *Top to bottom:*
Dianne Cousin on a balcony; Dianne
and her husband Manuel at their
wedding at her mother's apartment
in Lafitte; Dianne and Manuel's
son, Marlon, with his cousins on a
balcony. Photographs courtesy of
the Cousin family.

Dianne Cousin explained how her family used the Lafitte as a way to restabilize after Betsy as well:

When I moved in, I was 12 years old. I moved from the Lower Ninth Ward. We all lived with my grandmother. We owned a house down there. It was ruined in Hurricane Betsy, and my mama was a single parent. She applied for a housing unit and got one in 1969. There were five of us and my mom. She worked in the laundry at Charity Hospital. She worked hard and stood up all day. A lot of low-income people worked in the Quarter—in restaurants or some hotels.

According to the U.S. Department of Housing and Urban Development, families who spend more than 30% of their income on housing are at risk of not being able to afford other basic necessities like food, clothing, transportation, or medical care. Residents like Dianne's mother who worked for a state institution like Charity could count on some benefits, but people who worked in restaurants and hotels often lived below the poverty level with jobs that provided no health insurance or retirement. In an unstable service economy, public housing like the Lafitte provided housing security while effectively subsidizing the hotel industry. Although many families eventually moved out, the bricks became a metaphor of stability for many residents. They not only helped weather hurricanes in New Orleans, but also helped families through hard times, and provided a place they could count on when they were managing long-term illness or disability. Dwayne Brumfield is a long-term resident of the Lafitte whose family is from Franklinton in Washington Parish, Louisiana. Like many families from the country, his family had to go to New Orleans for medical care. His mother moved into Lafitte when he was young to help him with his medical condition. He said:

I was a seven-month premature baby. I have muscular dystrophy and cerebral palsy. I'm glad I'm alive.

I came to New Orleans to go into Children's Hospital to help me walk. I was six years old and had gone into first grade. I stayed at the hospital, off and on, until I was ten. There was a whole bunch of us—black and white. We all ate together and stuff like that.

My mother, Jessie, decided to move to New Orleans to be closer to the hospital. When I was 17, my mom, older brother, and I moved into Lafitte on 2600 Orleans Avenue. It was right after Hurricane Besty. My mother got sick off and on. She worked as a domestic worker when she could to help us survive. The way I got around at that time was on my crutches. I could get up and down the stairs in our apartment by going up them backward by lifting myself up on my own. I've been here ever since.

Left: Marion Longwood with her daughter Furtis. Photograph by Bruce Sunpie Barnes. *Right:* Lafitte's Scrubs football team. Photograph courtesy of Emelda Paul.

My mother tried to get me in a regular school, but the school didn't want to take responsibility for me going up and down stairs, so I had to go into special ed. At that time, under Louisiana law, special education only went until you were 16 and then you had to drop out. It made me mad. It's not that I didn't want to learn. The year after I had to stop school, they changed the law and started sending handicapped students to regular classes, but it was too late for me. I went to night school for a while, and I can read and write and take care of myself.

While some members of extended families in the Lafitte stayed for generations, others moved out and returned when loved ones became sick. Marion LeBlanc, for instance, moved into an apartment between North Johnson and Prieur in 1941. She raised her daughter, Diana, in the development. Diana moved out for more than 20 years, and then returned to take care of her father when he became sick. She now takes care of her mother.

ETHICS OF CARE

Caretaking in the Lafitte extended well beyond the nuclear family. The close-knit courtyards with shared porches and balconies encouraged neighbors get to know each other, and many residents helped each other with childcare. Jazz musician James Andrews grew up in the St. Peter Court, right next to the singer Johnny Adams. After his parents moved away, he often stayed with his grandmother, Dorothy Hill. He explained:

At times, we probably had 15 to 20 people in the apartment. And thank God she had it because it was probably the only place a bunch of family members had to go. Plus she'd cook every day. I still go by her house today to eat.

Like Dorothy, Marion Longwood minded a lot of children. One of the oldest residents in the Lafitte, she was born at home in 1915 at 2006 Conti Street, just on the uptown side of the Carondelet Canal, and was raised in Gerttown until the Lafitte was built. She moved back downtown with her family, and got married in the project a few years later. Throughout her life, however, she lived mostly with her parents, and helped support them by working as a hotel elevator operator. Her great joy was helping raise other children in the Lafitte. Marion said:

I wish I had a home to take them all in. If people don't want children, give them to people who want them. I raised kids but I didn't born them.

When she was 40 years old, she adopted her daughter, Furtis. Furtis explained, "She loves all kinds of kids. We all got along. Some call me sister." Although she had to leave school when she was young to help take care of her family, Marion stayed committed to school and volunteered at Phillis Wheatley Elementary for decades.

It wasn't just women who did this kind of caretaking. Men in and around the project were also involved. Bruce Davenport remembered how he looked up to the older boys and men in the project, and thought they set good examples:

In the Lafitte, you have a porch with three doors on it. On those porches, you have a group of kids. We all hung together, played ball together. You had those playgrounds and coaches were coming into the projects, taking the kids to show them something different. Bringing them to different places. They didn't become a gangster. A lot of those band directors and coaches were father figures to those kids—they'd tell them right from wrong.

One of the coaches who has been involved in the Lafitte community consistently over the years is Joe Cayou. While he was growing up in the Lafitte, athletics helped him move through the pain of not having his own father in his life. He explained:

I was a hell of an athlete when I was at Clark Senior High. I scored 38 points one time against Xavier Prep, but my father wasn't at the game. It hurt. I had 38 scholarships, and went to Grambling. I've done something to motivate these kids, too. I started a football league; bought trophies. Every Saturday we had a game. The Miro Court would play the Derbigny Court. The parents know when they put their kids in my hands, I'm going to take care of them like they're my own. The parents donated food. Some parents tell me now they are doing so good—"He's in college, he owes everything to you." That makes me feel good.

By living close to the the French Quarter and the Municipal Auditorium, young people also had a chance to get to know the wider world outside of the Lafitte. Michelle Nelson recalled:

Robert, Melvin, Herlin, and Lionel and I were called "Bang Bang the Project Gang." We played football right over in Lemann Park and in the big old Tonti Court. Every year in June, Barnum & Bailey Circus came to the Municipal Auditorium. That was it. Sometimes we worked to get in by feeding the elephants or walking the horses. I guess we were just little hustlers. Our moms couldn't afford for us to go otherwise.

James Andrews told the story of the beginning of his musical career:

My grandmother used to tell my cousin and me, "Y'all can go outside, but don't go too far." Some kind of way, we wind up in the French Quarter. We watched these kids from the St. Thomas Project tap dancing and how much money they're making. Next thing we're tap-dancing and Chris Owens is coming in the project looking for us. She wanted to hire us to come dance with her. My grandmother said, "Oh, no, that's not my grandchildren. They would never be out there tap dancing."
Chris said, "Yeah, that's them there now."
I said, "Oh no, we got trouble, boys." But my grandmother let us go. Chris bought us tuxedos and had us dancing. That's what really introduced me to the Quarter and all over New Orleans. And I really learned how to entertain.

Along the edge of Lafitte Street, there was a wide stretch of open land from where the Carondelet Canal was filled in. The Southern Railway ran along it, but the open space near North Claiborne was turned into Lemann Park by the New Orleans Recreational Department. Photograph of Lemann Park courtesy of the New Orleans Public Library's City Archives.

Left: The Square Deal in front of Dooky Chase's on Orleans Avenue. Photograph by Ralston Crawford, courtesy of the Hogan Jazz Archive. *Middle:* Guy LeBlanc in front of the closed Carver Theater. The Carver has since reopened as an event venue. Photograph by Bethany Rogers. *Right:* Walter's Place. Photograph by Ralston Crawford, courtesy of the Hogan Jazz Archive.

ENTERTAINING A NEIGHBORHOOD: ORLEANS AND CLAIBORNE

Orleans Street used to be like Canal Street. It was always crowded. At Easter time, you'd see the kids dressed up walking with their baskets. My friends and I sat on benches of the neutral ground of North Claiborne. —Paulette Clay

During segregation, black-owned businesses around the Lafitte created their own institutions that provided safe places that endeared themselves to their clientele and stayed in their hearts long after they closed. Leah Chase, an internationally recognized chef who has run a restaurant across from the Lafitte on Orleans Avenue for more than 50 years, remembered growing up with restaurants run by black women. Leah described the places:

They were not big spaces. A lot of them were bars, but those women ran good bars. I'm talking no nonsense bars. They went to them dressed in their little uniform and they always wore this pretty handkerchief in their pocket, and they made money and they hired people....There were a lot of women in the black community who had little spaces, where they had maybe one table, or maybe it was a takeout place. In the 1940s, I used to go to one—that lady just had a little stove and couple of little tables and she would cook the best butter beans I've ate in my life.

Joyce Giles lived in the Lafitte for 56 years. She raised eight children, working at Charity Hospital for over 30. But when she was 14 years old, she worked in a barroom that was later torn down when the interstate highway was built. Joyce remembered:

I was working as a waitress at Joe Prop's Plaza Bar on the corner of North Villere and St. Peter. We had certain uniforms we wore on the weekend. On Friday, we wore green. On Saturday, blue. And all during the week we wore white. They had one of them old-time record boxes. All kinds of people—white, black, Hispanic—came in there. We all had natural born fun, and swapped drinks no matter who was sitting at the table.

Harvey Reed remembered participating in the same kind of nights out in barrooms along North Claiborne. He had a circle of friends who would go out together wearing matching black coats and white pants. Harvey said:

Every time we'd have six of us go in there. They'd think we all have money, but we didn't. One night I might treat, the next night another might treat. That's it.

Harvey was also a member of the Square Deal Social and Pleasure Club. One of the oldest benevolent societies in downtown New Orleans, they were known for their second line parades where club mem-

Bruce Brice's mural by on a building in Tremé documents the demolition of part of the neighborhood.
Photograph by Michael P. Smith, courtesy of Bruce Brice.

bers wore dress pants, suspenders, and fancy hats. They carried baskets with baby dolls and cigars hanging from the sides, and inspired other clubs like the Sixth Ward Diamonds and the Tremé Sports that came after them.

In 1950, the Carver Theater, then considered one of the most modern black movie theaters in the country, opened on Orleans Avenue. Guy LeBlanc was a regular. He said:

I was born and raised in the middle of the Tonti Court. The whole Tonti know me. The whole court. They can't get rid of me. They can never take the place of me in the Tonti. I loved walking over to the Carver Theater. You just want to sit front and center, in the third row. Directly in the middle. Popcorn and cold drink, and that's it—I'm set. Carver closed in 1980. Been closed a long time. We missed our fun.

URBAN RENEWAL?

The 1960s brought in massive social and physical change to the Lafitte neighborhood. In 1964, the city spent 1.7 million dollars to buy land in the area of Tremé between North Rampart and North Claiborne for a cultural center that was modeled after the Lincoln Center in New York City. 122 families—all but one people of color—were displaced. Many of the residents in the area were forced to relocate to the Lafitte or public housing that was built across the river in the Fischer Projects. Uncle Lionel Batiste, who was the bass drummer for the Tremé Brass Band for many years, lived across the street from Craig Elementary on St. Philip Street. He learned to play the drum there, and later inspired students at the school who heard him practicing at home. When his house was torn down, Uncle Lionel moved to the Lafitte. Joyce Giles remembered seeing him in impromptu parades:

Top left: North Claiborne Avenue before the interstate was built. *Bottom left:* The construction of I-10 on North Claiborne. Photographs courtesy of the New Orleans Public Library's City Archives. *Top right:* A mural of LaBranche's pharmacy under the I-10 overpass by Mr. and Mrs. McCormick. Photograph by Rachel Breunlin. *Bottom right:* Uncle Lionel Batiste in St. Louis Cemetery No. 2 by North Claiborne. Photograph by Bruce Sunpie Barnes.

Those were the days, baby. You know the Dirty Dozen Kazoo Band was coming when they hit that tambourine—here they come! They could sing that Indian music just as good. Uncle Lionel could sing it really good. He was a nut.

During Carnival, Mardi Gras Indians used the neutral ground of North Claiborne as a meeting ground. Families gathered there to listen to them sing as they greeted each other in homemade suits or to watch the Zulu Social Aid and Pleasure Club pass through their neighborhood. The Black Arts writer Tom Dent wrote in 1977 in the *Black River Journal* that it was "the ubiquitous free 'front yard' of the Sixth and Seventh Wards, the city's bounteous gift to the community."

The gift was taken away in the 1960s. Using the Section 106 process around sites that qualified for the National Register of Historic Places, urban activists were able to prevent an interstate highway from going through the French Quarter. While this was a significant victory, North Claiborne Avenue, being a state-owned road and not under the same oversight, was chosen instead. Paulette Clay summarized the sentiment of many Lafitte residents,

The thing that really got me was when they put that I-10 up and took the trees and benches away. Guess that was supposed to be better—so they say.

Under the I-10 overpass on North Claiborne. Photograph by Michel Varisco.

The live oak trees, pillars of subtropical urbanity, were replaced with concrete that carried the roar of the highway overhead. Tom Dent lamented that the street underneath became:

a dustbowl, a wasteland untouched by sunlight or greenery, and the neighborhood around it has suffered from the abuse of massive automotive pollution and noise.

Long-standing businesses all along North Claiborne, including LaBranche's Pharmacy, closed. In the late 1970s, the Claiborne Avenue Design Team (CADT), organized by city planner and cofounder of Tambourine and Fan Rudy Lombard, worked with the surrounding neighborhoods to create a plan to revitalize the corridor. Although the published CADT document continues to be cited as an important response to urban renewal, only a few parts of the plan that were implemented. In collaboration with Tambourine and Fan, Hunter's Field Park was created in the Seventh Ward. A few decades later, Mayor Marc Morial's administration supported artists to paint murals dedicated to local history and culture on the columns under the highway.

New Orleans, Louisiana
June 15, 1955

A. P. TUREAUD
ATTORNEY AND COUNSELOR-AT-LAW
CLAVER BLDG., 1821 ORLEANS AVE.
NEW ORLEANS 16, LA.

June 16, 1955

Orleans Parish School Board
701 Carondelet Street
New Orleans, Louisiana

Gentlemen:

I enclose herewith petitions
signed by various persons who are
parents of Negro children attending the
public schools of this city, requesting
that full force and effect be immediately
given to the decisions of the United
States Supreme Court of May 17, 1954 and
May 31, 1955.

As attorney for these parents,
I shall be pleased to make myself available to your Honorable Board for any
conference or discussion of this petition.

Very truly yours,

A. P. Tureaud

APT:jcl

Enc.

Letter written by civil rights attorney A.P. Tureaud from his office in the Knights of St. Peter Claver building (formerly the French Hospital) across from the Lafitte on Orleans Avenue. Ernest "Dutch" Morial, another civil rights attorney who became mayor, also had an office in the building. His son Jacques recalls learning how to play baseball in the courtyards of the project. Correspondence courtesy of the Orleans Parish School Board Collection at the University of New Orleans' Louisiana Collection.

DESEGREGATING SCHOOLS

While the city dramatically changed the physical landscape around the Lafitte, the Civil Rights Movement was calling for an end to *de jure* segregation. Organizers were meeting throughout the Sixth Ward in places like the Knights of St. Peter Claver (formerly the French Hospital), Mount Zion Baptist Church, Dooky Chase's restaurant, and the home of Oretha and Doris Castle on North Tonti Street to organize legal attacks and nonviolent resistance to the laws.

All through the 1950s and 1960s, white officials in power in New Orleans city government enacted policies to reinforce segregation and unequal access to education. It took decades for middle and high school education to be funded again for black students. McDonogh 35 on South Rampart Street

Left: Phillis Wheatley Elementary School when it was first built. Raised on concrete piers, the design gave the impression that the building was floating. It was considered one of the modernist architectural gems in the city until the school board replaced the glass windows with cheap colored plexiglass. Photograph by Frank Lotz Miller, courtesy of the Southeastern Architectural Archive at Tulane University. *Right:* A photograph of children from Phillis Weatley performing for the Lafitte Residential Council meeting from a HANO annual report in 1981, courtesy of the New Orleans Public Library's City Archives.

was the only high school for black students until the school board turned the old Bayou Road School into another high school in 1947, renaming it Joseph S. Clark. Milton Batiste, the assistant leader of the Olympia Brass Band, remembered there were so many students in the "pioneering" class that they had to go to school on a platoon system. In 1951, a white elementary school in Tremé was handed down to black students for a middle school and renamed McDonogh 41 before it was torn down to build the "cultural complex." As a replacement, the school board turned a Catholic girls' school on Ursulines Street—across from the St. Ann shrine and right next to a white middle school—into a junior high school for black children called Andrew J. Bell.

In 1954, the United States' Supreme Court verdict in *Brown v. Board of Education* declared "separate but equal" unconstitutional, and ordered for public schools around the United States to be desegregated with all deliberate speed. However, when the desegregation orders came through from the federal courts, Orleans Parish went ahead with its plans to build more segregated schools, and tore down two acres of housing a few blocks away from the Lafitte on Dumaine Street to build Phillis Wheatley Elementary for black children. Charles R. Colbert, the school board's architect and planner, designed a school that was supposed to be built for 800 pupils, with only a sixth of the recommended amount of space. He raised the building on concrete piers to create room underneath the school for children to play.

It wasn't until the late 1960s that public schools desegregated. When the school board did require integration, it went only one direction. Clark Senior High, for instance, did not integrate white students into its school, but John McDonogh Senior High (often shortened to "John Mac") opened its doors to black students. Within five years, the student body of John Mac flipped from all white to nearly all black. As during the era of Reconstruction, the school board's commitment to integration did not go very deep.

MUSIC AND PARADES AS PARTICIPATION

Music was an important part of young people from the Lafitte's educational experiences. In the early 1950s, Ms. Yvonne Busch, a trombone player who had been the only female musician in Southern University's jazz band, was the music teacher for many of the schools they attended. At Clark, she ran a tight ship, winning a state championship and teaching students like Smokey Johnson and James Black who went on to be well-known musicians. A drum cadence that Smokey made up in her classroom, "Ratty #9," became the introduction to the song "It Ain't My Fault." The Olympia Brass Band adopted it, and their version became a popular number at second lines around the neighborhood.

In 1967, the elite white Carnival club, Rex, hired St. Augustine's marching band to perform in their Mardi Gras parade. The move was the first step in transforming the youth culture of marching bands around the city. Over the next few years, as city schools began to integrate, more and more students got to experience the huge swell of crowds during the carnival parades. Young people from the Lafitte, who had gone to Bell Junior High, could decide whether they wanted to go to Clark or John Mac. Both were located on Esplanade Avenue, and rivalry between the marching bands developed. Students at John Mac's were known for their dance, "The Mac Attack," and their boast, "Ace of Spade, Deuce of Spade, We Rule Esplanade!"

The leader of the Soul Rebels Brass Band, Lumar Allen, learned to play brass band music as part of Milton Batiste's Young Olympia Brass Band:

Top: Andrew J. Bell after Hurricane Katrina and Bruce Davenport holding a drawing he did of the Bell marching band. Photographs by Bruce Sunpie Barnes. *Botom:* The Bell band in the 1960s, courtesy of Joseph Torregano.

Top: Mardi Gras parades going down Orleans Avenue. Photographs courtesy of Parreletta Carter. *Bottom:* The Zulu Social Aid and Pleasure Club under the I-10 overpass at Orleans and Claiborne. Photograph by Rachel Breunlin.

That music scene was big. So many kids were carrying instruments, wanting to be in the band. The band director of Bell, Donald Richard, had everybody's attention in that community. Their band would always be heard. Everybody had a horn or drum, and I was into that.

Bruce Davenport explained the power of participating in the local school cultures of sports and music, and then creating his own art:

Participating in something protects you. If you had talent, you try to use it. Some kids were brought up with an instrument in their hand. Some kids were brought up with a gun in their hand. I was brought up with an ink pen and a football in my hand, so that's what I deal with. I used to draw different scenes on the project walls.

In the 1990s, the principal of John Mac was a member of the Zulu Social Aid & Pleasure Club. During the parade, the band played in front of his float, getting to march past the Lafitte on Orleans Avenue and under the I-10 expressway at North Claiborne. The Lafitte apartments that ran along Orleans were prized for their Mardi Gras location. Tapica Sparkman explained why she loved her apartment:

It was upstairs and down, and I had my own little balcony. At Mardi Gras, family members might sleep in the living room or the kitchen just to get their spot at six in the morning—to get right on the corner in front of the crowd. Some might be out there overnight!

HANO NEWS

Vol. 2 No. 1   December, 1976   New Orleans, LA

Community Vegetable Garden Planted

Harold Bordenave, a Lafitte resident, is responsible for obtaining and maintaining a vegetable garden for use by all residents of public housing.

After selecting the site for the garden, Bordenave had to wade through a maze of red tape to find the owner so as to acquire the land.

Eventually with the help and guidance of Emelda Washington of the Catholic Archdiocese and members of the Parkway Commission, Bordenave was able to acquire the property (as a

representative of HANO) from the Parkway Commission.

To help the garden get off to a good start, the land was initially cultivated and fertilized by members of the Parkway Commission before actual planting began.

The plot of land used for the garden is located in the 2100 block of Lafitte Street, is 65 feet by 700 feet, and is surrounded by a seven-foot fence.

Individual plots are measured off at 15 feet each, and are available to all residents of public housing. However, because the space is limited, the garden can only accommodate 100 individual spaces.

At present, the garden is mostly being utilized by senior citizens of the Lafitte

(continued on page 6)

Harold Bordenave, left, and helper Willie Robinson, right, carefully check progress of a cotton bush that has grown successfully in a garden especially set aside for public housing residents.

Harold Bordenave, a Lafitte resident and co-ordinator of a vegetable garden for all public housing residents, diligently checks some of his crops. The garden, which has space available for 100 individual plots, presently consists of bountiful crops of tomatoes, okra, collard and mustard greens, pole beans and lettuce.

EDITOR'S NOTE. The HANO NEWS will be published by and for the employees and tenants of this Authority. It does not supplement or alter this Authority's official manuals, administrative rules and regulations. Anything of an official nature will be so labeled.

In the mid-1970s, a Lafitte resident, Harold Bordenave, successfully campaigned for part of the land on the 2100 block of Lafitte Street (formerly the Carondelet Canal) to be set aside as a community garden for residents of public housing. Image from *HANO News* in 1977.

SELF-REPRESENTATION

The Civil Rights Movement had an impact on public housing. Official desegregation came slowly, and was implemented only in the two white developments, Iberville and St. Thomas, where black families were allowed to rent apartments. White families did not move into developments like the Lafitte that had originally been designated as "colored."

In the 1970s, Jim Hayes and Ron Chisom set up the Tremé Community Improvement Association in an apartment in the Lafitte at 808 Orleans Avenue. Inspired by national tenants' rights movements, they used popular education models to connect the rights of public housing residents to broader issues of affordable housing in the surrounding neighborhood. These collective efforts led to the Lafitte becoming the first residential council in the city to begin sharing decision-making with HANO. The sharing of power did not come without a fight. Leah Green, former president of the residential council, said:

HANO always believed that the residents shouldn't have no say so. The residents shouldn't have governance over anything. But we thought different, you understand. Without residents, HANO wouldn't have a job.

Just as residents were beginning to restructure how public housing was administered, the Reagan Administration began to slash the HUD's budget. In the 1980s, eighty percent of public housing funding was cut. Social services and youth programming that used to be a core part of the Department of Housing and Urban Development's budget were no longer available. Very little money was designated for the repair of apartment buildings. The "one for one" replacement law meant that for every unit that was torn down, another had to be built. But the law made no provision for empty units. Facing draconian budget cuts, housing officials let an increasing number of units fall into disrepair and remain vacant.

Along with major changes in the physical area around the Lafitte, the economy of the city was changing dramatically, too. Shipping technology moved to containers, and the "river work" that was the livelihood of so many people in the city disappeared. Small businesses along Claiborne and Orleans had been torn down for the highway expansion. In areas with fewer economic opportunities, the underground drug trade took hold, and with it, an escalation in violence to protect drug dealing territory. The Lafitte wasn't spared. Lumar Allen explains how this impacted day-to-day life:

When that crack came in in the 1980s, you could see it changing. We used to have a milkman in the 1970s. Man used to actually come and take your order, and bring your milk. But see, they started robbing the truck. You know, he had cash on him. We used to walk to church at St. Peter Claver. My aunts and my mom went to the early mass at 7:30. It might be dark, but it was no problem. When the '80s came, you could see people hanging around there that had that look in their eyes. The old ladies started going to mass at a different time.

Although crime rates in public housing were not necessarily higher than the surrounding neighborhoods, the physical layout of the community built around courtyards and without many thoroughfares made the project a kind of island—distinct, but also not a place that people visited unless they knew someone who lived there.

Hope Bland explained the difference between living on Orleans Avenue and in one of the couryards:

A sign protesting violence in the Lafitte in 2004. Photograph by Ashley Nelson.

On the Avenue, your door is right there. If I was going to have company, my company could park their car right outside my door—just like a house. As far as the courtyard, you have to come to the driveway and park out there. I'll give you another example. Cabs. I can get a cab on the Avenue like that. I can't get a cab in the court, because they're not coming to the driveway at night. At all, period. I guess it's the feel of actually having to come in the projects. The good have to suffer for the bad.

City-wide, there became a vague, stereotypical idea of who lived in public housing. Dianne Cousin worked at Loyola University as a administrative assistant for more than 30 years. She went to college there and has also helped her kids through school. She explained how people react when she she grew up in the Lafitte:

They can't believe it, but I did. I'm not ashamed to say it, but I didn't want to live there for the rest of my life.

Although many people have seen public housing as a stepping-stone to another form of housing, one of the main reasons people wanted to leave was because of the violence they couldn't get away from. Being an "outside" or "inside" person often depended on how you dealt with the possibility of random violence. Joyce Giles reflected:

I loved my porch. I sat on it 24/7 and I saw too much. But if they wouldn't put it out there, I wouldn't have seen it. I wasn't worried, and I'm not scared of none of them.

What did she see? Ricky B started freestyling at John Mac in the 1980s, and went on to document life in different public housing developments around the city in his raps. In "Shake Fo Yo Hood," he calls out the Lafitte:

I'm on Claiborne by the Lafitte
I hear shots ring on the other end
By the Rocheblave Court
But on Miro somebody dead from a bullet wound
Read about it in The Times Picayune, murder rate: Boom!

The Soul Rebels Brass Band, circa mid-1990s. Photograph by Ed Newman.

Ricky B reflected later:

If I'm going to rep the city, I want to rep it right. We can look at the news all day and find what's really going on, but if you really want to get to the core of what this city's about, talk to the people who lived in it and experienced it. We survived 1993 to 1999—the worst time in the city. And you know, we're still here, doing something positive.

Bruce Davenport also used art to confront the violence:

I couldn't hang outside too late because these little fools out here were shooting. I'd go home and draw stuff happening in the project—stuff like robberies and murders. My grandmother said, "Don't draw that no more."

Bruce's grandmother's concern came from a number of angles. She was worried that the violence was impacting her grandson's mental health, but she was also concerned about how representing the violence would be perceived by the people who were perpetuating it. Often people who committed violent crime in the Lafitte knew their neighbors had witnessed, or were aware of, what they had done. Living so close together with these truths was its own form of terrorism. Wanda Dubose explained, "You're afraid to speak out because of the drugs. You more or less quiet. Nobody wants to get their house shot up and nobody wants to get shot up."

Like other times in the history of New Orleans, music became another way of speaking. Lumar recalls that, "a lot of people—a lot of young people— were dying. We were playing funerals, not only every week, at least four times a week." The Soul Rebels responded to the violence by writing a song called "Let Your Mind Be Free." Lumar said:

When the Soul Rebels started, we wanted to be this "fight the power" type of group. That's where the fatigues came in, the black shirt like Public Enemy. The violence had escalated in the 90s, so we wanted to make a song that said "Stop the killing." "Let Your Mind Be Free" was made from that impetus.

Members of the Lafitte Residential Council in 2005 standing in front of the Sojourner Truth Community Center. *Left to right:* Leah Green, Florence Slack, Stella Carr, and Emelda Paul. Photograph courtesy of the Neighborhood Story Project.

The Lafitte Residential Council responded to the increase in violence as well. They worked with HANO to create a community center in part of the area that used to be the Carondelet Canal. Former Residential Council president Emelda Paul explained:

We called it Sojourner Truth. She was a lady. She was a slave. She was on a mission. She was on a journey. We were women who were on a journey. We're still on a journey.

Mayor Marc Morial—son of Ernest "Dutch" Morial (who used to have his law practice across from the Lafitte at the Knights of St. Peter Claver)—helped HANO purchase the land for one dollar to build the Sojourner Truth Community Center. When the contractor for the building decided to install garage doors in the main meeting room, the Residential Council went on strike and blocked the doors to the building to prevent further construction until an agreement was made that it would be a more inviting entryway. The ribbon cutting was in 2000.

In 2004, the Neighborhood Story Project began running a collaborative ethnography project at John McDonogh Senior High. Over that school year, we worked closely with Ashley Nelson and her family on a book about the Lafitte. Although she was the third generation in her family to live in the project, she initially had a lot of trouble when she asked her friends and neighbors to participate in the book project. She wrote,

I'd approach people with kindness and they'd be all for it until I told them about release forms and showed them the tape recorder. Then it "No, baby, I'm not bout to get on no tape" or "I don't know nothing about back here."

The brick and cinder block rubble of the "new" section of C.J. Peete (formerly the Magnolia) Public Housing Development, built with federal funds from the Housing Act of 1949, and torn down in 2004–2005. Photograph by Michel Varisco.

Eventually, as people read more stories Ashley had written and saw some of the ways the interviews were coming together, they began to participate in the book project, and in 2005 it was published as *The Combination*. In her introduction, she spoke directly to the issues of isolation:

You wouldn't see someone from the suburbs just walking through saying, "Oh, I was just in the neighborhood, thought I'd swing by." We do have problems in Lafitte, but damn, it doesn't mean you have to run away from us. The world has problems and we are all a part of them somehow, even if people don't want to admit it.

Ashley's point—that problems in public housing are connected to broader structural issues in American society—comes into fuller light when individual developments are understood within the context of national housing policy.

WHAT IS THE FUTURE OF PUBLIC HOUSING?

For many years, the United States Congress has not allocated enough money for the maintenance and upkeep of public housing developments all over the country. According to the Council of Large Public Housing Authorities, from 1995 to 2008, the country lost 165,000 public housing units from delayed maintenance. Other housing units have stayed vacant or have been seen as causing major health problems. For instance, New Orleans has extremely high rates of lead in households all over the city, but public housing was particularly contaminated because all the paint originally used in the developments contained lead and the units were never remediated. A class action lawsuit, *Billieson v. City of New Orleans, et al*, was filed on behalf of families with children who suffered lead poisoning from living in, or visiting public housing from 1987 to early 2001. In 2013, HANO insurance companies agreed to a $67 million settlement. By that time, most of the developments involved in the lawsuit, including the Lafitte, were closed.

The process of redeveloping public housing began in 1992 when Congress passed an amendment to the National Housing Act to remove the "one for one replacement" law, which required that every unit of public housing that was torn down be replaced. Soon afterwards, HUD created the HOPE VI Program, which tore down old developments and replaced them with housing designed fit into the broader neighborhoods. In New Orleans in the late 1990s and early 2000s, the St. Thomas, Desire, Florida, and parts of C.J. Peete (the Magnolia) and Guste Housing Developments were torn down. Mary Johnson had moved into the St. Thomas when her mother passed away in 1977. She described the process of relocating:

When they began tearing St. Thomas down, we had to find somewhere else to live, and they relocated me to the Lafitte. I was in the Tonti Court when I first moved in. They called it the Wild Side, On the other side of Galvez was the Real Side. And it was—there was guns and drugs. You name it, then they had it. But St. Thomas wasn't no better.

Tapica Sparkman had also grown up in public housing uptown in the Magnolia Project. She decided to raise her own family in the Lafitte:

In 1993, I moved on Galvez and Orleans. I moved because I wanted to get out on my own with my family. At that time, I was married and my son was three. When the Sojourner Truth Community Center opened, they had nice classes for us to take. I was a childcare teacher, and took a childcare class.

Like Mary and Tapica, many families had to balance their concerns about safety and their need for affordable housing. However, most residents were not aware that HANO and HUD were drafting plans to redevelop the project as well.

Detail of mural of the Lafitte Public Housing Development after Hurricane Katrina by Bruce Davenport.

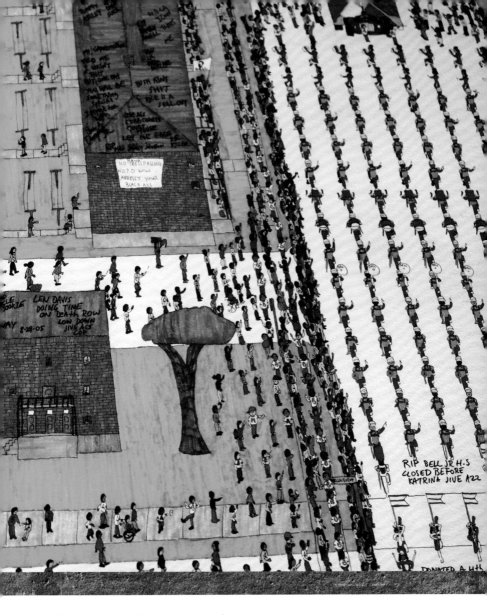

Rebuilding Again

Left: Floodwater in Lafitte after Hurricane Katrina. Photograph courtesy of Mary Moore. *Right:* Evacuation out of New Orleans in the days after Katrina. Many families found saftey on the I-10 overpass. Photograph courtesy of Mary Moore.

HURRICANE KATRINA

The bricks that were used to build the Lafitte came from the clay pulled out of Lake Pontchartrain. On August 29, 2005, the water from the lake broke through the drainage canals around New Orleans. Water gushed into the streets and slowly filled up more than 80 percent of the city, including parts of the Lafitte. Michelle Nelson stayed for the storm. He explained:

During Katrina, those projects they really helped us out. They helped me with my mom and my family. I think we would've died. I had somewhere to shelter them. Even though we didn't have any lights, we had gas. I was able to cook. When water got into my mom's unit on Orleans, we moved to a different apartment. I started helping transport people out with a boat and got separated from her. She was taken to Houston and I was taken to Arkansas.

Many families in the Lafitte had similar experiences of being separated from loved ones and finding themselves in unfamiliar states. Houston's Astrodome, where one of the largest concentrations of Katrina evacuees found shelter, was full of Lafitte residents who had posted names of loved ones they couldn't locate on notice boards. It took weeks, and sometimes months, for people to reunite. At that point, the floodwaters in the city had been pumped out, and the incredible damage was being assessed. Residents of New Orleans from all racial and economic backgrounds experienced a deep sense of exile as they wanted to return home, but many couldn't because their homes were flooded. For public housing residents who did not have control over whether their homes would be reopened by HANO, this feeling was particularly cutting. Joe Cayou recounts his first time back in the city:

When we came back from Houston on the interstate, I cried like a baby when I saw what I saw. I couldn't believe that the place that I lived in all my life and loved so much was looking the way it looked. And when I found out they were going to tear it down, I was broke down.

Within six months of the storm, news began spreading that four of the biggest public housing developments in the city—the Lafitte, C.J. Peete (the Magnolia), B.W. Cooper (the Calliope), and the St. Bernard—wouldn't be reopened. Local and national housing activists questioned the legality of keeping such large amounts of affordable housing closed when so many people had been displaced by the storm. International lawyers convened to investigate whether it breached the United Nations' policies on internally displaced peoples' right to return.

All over the region, conferences, charrettes, and other meetings were taking place to make plans for rebuilding. At the Gulf Coast Reconstruction Conference, the Yes Men—a culture jamming, satirical organization that uses mock press conferences to generate discussions about top-down corporate and government policies around the world—gave a speech. A member of the organization posed as a representative of Alphonso Jackson, and announced that HUD would "reopen all housing projects in New Orleans and allow these Americans to be part of their city again." Following the speech, a ribbon cutting was held at the Lafitte to symbolize a new direction. Residents were excited about the 180-degree change before the stunt was revealed. HUD's spokeswoman, Donna White, came out with a rebuttal:

It is terribly sad that someone would perpetrate such a cruel hoax and play on the fears and anxieties of families who are desperate to return to their homes. We are destroying those homes for good reason....It is terribly sad that some people can't understand that. That lack of understanding speaks for the low level of government education in this country.

It's true that many people do not know the history of public housing in the United States or follow national legislation around affordable housing policy. A 2013 HUD report found that renters who had "worst case housing needs" and had not received housing subsidies increased from 7.1 million to 8.5 million between 2009 and 2011. And yet, Congress cut spending on public housing by 20 percent, making it extremely difficult for local housing authorities to be able to keep up with maintenance, let alone be able to support others who have been on waiting lists for more than 10 years.

In New Orleans after Hurricane Katrina, HUD worked with HANO to request an expedited Section 106 review process for demolition and redevelopment. Historic preservationists who were part of the meetings recall that the decision to tear down had already been made by HUD with funding sources tied to demolition. In fact, when the city's Historic Conservation District Review Committee rejected HANO's application to demolish the Lafitte, HUD Secretary Alphonso Jackson sent a letter in December of 2007 to Mayor C. Ray Nagin encouraging him to overturn the decision or risk, according to HUD:

The loss of approximately $137 million in funds specifically to create affordable housing;
The loss of nearly 900 vouchers for Lafitte tenants requiring them to make their own rent payments; and
The loss of the 94 units of rehabilitated affordable housing previously agreed to as part of phased redevelopment.

Meanwhile, a coalition of public housing activists began to work with local lawyers to file a class action lawsuit against the decision to tear down the developments, and began occupying the St. Benard Housing Development. Eventually, housing activists forced the New Orleans City Council to vote on whether it would accept federal funding for the demolition of public housing. The decision was unanimous in favor of moving forward with redevelopment.

FAUBOURG LAFITTE

The redevelopment of public housing in New Orleans is based on public/private partnerships where public land and dollars are used to contract with private for-profit and nonprofit developers who are responsible for the construction and management of the new developments. In the case of the Lafitte, the contract for redevelopment was awarded to Providence Community Housing, Enterprise Community Housing, and L+M Development Partners. Building a new neighborhood in a politically charged environment is not easy. Working with Catholic Charities, the team reached out to Lafitte residents to help weave them into the redevelopment plans, and to explain the process of coming back to the new development. Providence-Enterprise has committed to a one-for-one replacement of public housing units in and around Faubourg Lafitte. In constructing the new development, they preserved the old live oak trees that were landmarks of the different courtyards, and built a combination of single-family homes and apartment buildings along the street grids of the surrounding neighborhood. A new street called "Magic Street"—named by children from the Lafitte—now runs through the middle of the neighborhood. Along the old Carondelet Canal, one of the Claiborne Avenue Design Team's planning recommendations from the 1970s to create a linear park from Bayou St. John to the French Quarter is finally emerging as the Lafitte Greenway.

Along with the physical landscape of the neighborhood, the fine art of porch-sitting has also been reconfigured. Smaller porches, rules about how many residents can congregate outside at one time, and curfews for children keep the neighborhood quieter than it used to be. Parreletta Carter reflected:

In the new Lafitte, I miss my porch. Ain't no porch around here. But I like my place. If another hurricane comes, I ain't going nowhere. Can't go nowhere. The only way I'm going to move is if Jesus comes and gets me. It ain't gonna be too long. I'm tired of moving.

The redevelopment follows a widespread pattern of "urban restructuring" that has dramatically changed public health and education in the city as well. One of the new residents of Lafitte, Oscar Jiles, reflected:

Man, New Orleans is so different from the times I grew up. I sound old—cause I'm only 23! The neighborhoods are different, the schools are different, the projects are different. You'd see a lot of kids—me included—playing from sun-up to sundown. You hardly see that any more. Parents are scared to let their kids hang out as late as we used to—but you can't blame them with the guns and shootings.

Left: Planning meeting for Faubourg Lafitte at St. Peter Claver Catholic Church. Photograph courtesy of Nicole Swerhun. *Right:* Emelda Paul (*far right*) joins Mayor Ray Nagin and others at the groundbreaking for the new development. Photograph courtesy of Emelda Paul.

Left to right: Crossing guard Mary Moore with Faubourg Lafitte residents Lawrence Travis, E'mond Davis, and Aaron Davis; Mary helping the children cross Orleans Avenue, which is still wide from the days of the Orleans Canal (Dooky Chase's in the background); the new Phillis Wheatley building.

A brief survey of the public schools in the area shows that Oscar's point is well-taken. After a long battle between historic preservationists and the Recovery School District (with former residents on both sides), the midcentury modern Phillis Wheatley Elementary School was torn down and replaced with a new building. Andrew J. Bell Junior High did not reopen and may be turned into affordable artist lofts. Clark Senior High was chartered to FirstLine, which started the first charter school in New Orleans in 1998 and expanded to run a number of schools after the storm. The other public high school in the area, John McDonogh Senior High, has also been a site of great debate around urban restructuring. The Recovery School District issued a charter to an organization out of California called Future Is Now. Their attempt at reform was featured on a reality TV series called *Blackboard Wars* on the Oprah Winfrey Network. Community activists protested the school's involvement in the program after advertising claimed the series was a look into "one of the most dangerous schools in America." A year later, the school was closed due to low enrollment.

Faubourg Lafitte resident Michelle Nelson went to Wheatley, Bell, and John McDonogh. He has vivid memories of an annual parade when school kids stepped to the Bell band and threw Mardi Gras beads to neighbors. In sixth grade, he directed younger students across St. Ann Street while working as a patrol guard under the guidance of his favorite teacher, Mr. Grand Prix. He explained how he felt about the changes:

They're just removing all memory. They've taken all the places where I grew up. Now they're tearing down the school. When you said Phillis Wheatley, you said Lafitte.

In 2015, Mary Moore, a former resident of the Lafitte, is employed as a crossing guard by FirstLine, the charter that now operates the new Phillis Wheatley. Every morning, she waits for 11 children from Faubourg Lafitte to help them get to school, but notes that there are many other young people who board buses to go to schools all over the city. She says she loves her job, but "I miss the old timers. They'd be in their windows or on their porches letting people know what's what."

CALLING IT HOME

It wasn't just older residents of the Lafitte who decided not to return. Tapica Sparkman explained:

It's still a good place in the community to stay in, but I just don't want to go back. I want to go forward. I live in in a single home for me and my family in New Orleans East, and it's comfortable. I really like it, and work for the Lafitte at the Sojourner Truth Neighborhood Center.

Mary Johnson decided to return to Faubourg Lafitte. She said:

Everybody is more unto themselves now. I was glad to come back, but I prefer the bricks. I just miss my apartment, period—coming through that cut to 697 Tonti. I'll never forget that address.

After living in Faubourg Lafitte for a few years, Emelda Paul reflected on the memory of the old development in the new:

After Katrina and when the people were demolishing the Lafitte, I got a lot [of bricks]. There were a lot of friends who didn't have them, and they said, "Oh, Emelda, please give me one." Some of them put their name on them and the date, where they came from. I still have a few I've kept for myself. I think about the old buildings many times. I remember I would decorate the bricks with the lights for Christmas, and I'd follow the lines of the brick and mortar. I gave bricks to my daughters. I said, "Here, build your own Lafitte."

Walking through Faubourg Lafitte, the 19th century urban planning of Faubourg Tremé can still be seen in the wide neutral ground of Orleans Avenue, and linear park of the Lafitte Greenway. In the middle of the new street grid, a few buildings from the Lafitte Public Housing Development are being renovated into a Head Start Center. Nearby, mosaic artist Laurel True is working with residents to build a brick archway to connect the histories of Faubourg Tremé, the Lafitte Public Housing Development, and Faubourg Lafitte. In the plans, there are benches surrounding it. It will hopefully not just be a site of memory, but a new place to gather as well.

Left: Across from Faubourg Lafitte, young boys play soccer on the land that was once the Carondelet Canal. The land is being turned into a park called the Lafitte Greenway. Photograph by Austin Shea, courtesy of Providence Community Housing. *Right:* Jazz funeral for Travis "Trumpet Hill" Black on May 23, 2015 began at the Carver Theater and went down Orleans Avenue by Faubourg Lafitte. Travis, whose grandparents are Dorothy and Jesse Hill, grew up playing music in the courtyards of the Lafitte. A well-regarded trumpet player who led Trumpet Black and the Heart Attacks and was a member of the New Birth and New Breed Brass Bands, he died unexpectedly while playing music in Japan. Photograph by Bruce Sunpie Barnes.

Works Cited

Research for the Section 106 process was a collaborative effort. Oral histories were conducted by Bethany Rogers and Royce Osborn, and historical research was conducted by Dayna Bowker Lee and Rachel Breunlin. This research was supplemented by interviews and ethnography supervised by Rachel for the Neighborhood Story Project's book The Combination, *by Ashley Nelson. Historical archaeological research was generously provided by Ryan Gray and investigative reporting was shared by Katy Reckdahl. Unless otherwise cited here, all quotes are from the oral histories conducted for this project.*

INTRODUCTION

- Double Dutch rhyme from Katy Reckdahl's "Like a Ton of Bricks," published in *The Gambit Weekly* on October 24, 2006: www.bestofneworleans.com/gambit/like-a-ton-of-bricks/Content?oid+1246593

- For more on urban renewal in the 1960s, see Jane Jacobs' *The Death and Life of Great American Cities.* New York: Vintage, 1992. For a discussion of how "urban renewal" has been argued to be "black removal," see *Race, Culture, and the City: A Pedagogy for Black Urban Struggle*, by Stephen Nathan Haymes. New York: SUNY Press, 1995.

- For more on the Section 106 process and the Historic Preservation Act of 1966, see the Advisory Council on Historic Preservation's *Protecting Historic Properties: A Citizen's Guide to the Section 106 Review*, which can be accessed at: http://www.achp.gov/docs/CitizenGuide.pdf

- On "root shock," see Mindy Thompson Fullilove's *Root Shock: How Tearing Up City Neighborhoods Hurts America and What We Can Do About It.* United States: Ballantine Books, 2005.

- The Louisiana Creole proverb *Chatte brilé di feu* [A burnt cat dreads the fire] comes from Lafcadio Hearn's *Gombo Zhebes: A Little Dictionary of Creole Proverbs.* Boston: Applewood Books, 2001: 15.

BRICKS

- Sol Rosenthal, Jack J.H. Kessels, and Ernest W. Jones, Architects' 1939 *Specifications for the Construction of the Lafitte Avenue Housing Project, New Orleans, Louisiana. Project No. 1-5* can be found at the Southeastern Architectural Archive at Tulane University.

- Thanks to Katy Reckdahl for sharing Ferdinand Bigard's application to the National Register for Historic Places.

- Research on the brickyard on Bayou Road comes from Roulhac Toledano, Mary Louise Christovich, Robin Derbes, and Betsy Swanson's *New Orleans Architecture: Tremé and the Bayou Road.* New Orleans: Pelican Publishing, 2003: 9.

- Excerpt from Brenda Marie Osbey's poem "Faubourg" comes from *All Saints.* Baton Rouge: Louisiana State University Press, 1997: 37.

- Quotes from Rudy Hutchinson and Wilbert F. Monette on brick masonry in New Orleans come from the oral history project led by Nick Spitzer for an exhibit at the New Orleans Museum of Art called from *Raised to the Trade: Creole Building Arts of New Orleans*. A catalog of the exhibit was edited by John Ethan Hankins and Steven Maklansky and published by Pelican Publishing Company, 2003. Thanks to Laura Westbrook for helping us work with the archive.

- Quote about the Schneider Brick and Tile Company was found in the final report of principal investigator R. Christopher Goodwin's 1990 *Cultural Resources Survey of Gretna Levee Enlargement Item M-99.4 to 95.5-R Jefferson Parish, Louisiana.* New Orleans: U.S. Army Corps of Engineers: 99.

- On "honest" bricks, see Richard Sennett's *The Craftsman*. New Haven: Yale University Press, 2008: 136–137.

- The history of Tambourine and Fan and Jerome Smith's quote come from Bruce Sunpie Barnes and Rachel Breunlin's *Talk That Music Talk: Passing On Brass Band Music the Traditional Way*. New Orleans: The Center for the Book at the University of New Orleans, 2014: 30.

- Shirley Simmons' quote comes from Reckdahl's "Like A Ton of Bricks."

- Nicolai Ouroussoff's piece, "All Fall Down" was published in the *The New York Times* on November 19, 2006.

- Providence Community Housing executive director Jim Kelly quotes the All Congregations Together survey in Reckhal's "Like a Ton of Bricks."

- For more discussion on the plans to redevelop the Lafitte prior to Katrina, see the August 15, 2006 draft of the Housing Authority of New Orleans' "Physical Asset Recovery Plan."

HISTORY OF A BACK-A-TOWN NEIGHBORHOOD

- On the history of the Bayou Road and the Carondelet Canal, see Ari Kelman's 2006 *A River and Its City: The Nature of Landscape in New Orleans*. Berkeley: University of California Press; Toledano and Christovich 2003: 62-63; and Marcel Giraud's 1991 *A History of French Louisiana Volume V: The Company of the Indies, 1723–1731*, translated by Brian Pearce. Baton Rouge: Louisiana University Press. Other historical research compiled in Bowker Lee's unpublished report "Historic Overview of the Tremé-Lafitte Neighborhood."

- In "Expanding and Draining New Orleans," city statistics and drainage information, as well as a reconstruction of what the emerging Tremé-Lafitte neighborhood looked like comes from Bowker Lee.

- On the Third Municipality's response to the flood of 1849, see Harry Kmen's 1957 "New Orleans Forty Days in '49 in *Louisiana Historical Quarterly* 40(1): 25–45, and also Bowker Lee's research.

- In constructing the map of the block bounded by North Johnson, St. Peter, North Prieur, and Orleans, Ryan Gray correlated archaeological findings and census data. See his paper: "Re-Racing the Superblock: Spatial Contradictions and Slum Clearance at the Lafitte Public Housing Project, New Orleans, Louisiana."

- Quote about Thomy Lafon's philanthropy comes from Rodolphe Lucien Desdunes' 2001 *Our People and Our History: Fifty Creole Portraits*, translated from the French and edited by Sister Dorothea Olga McCants, Daughter of the Cross. Baton Rouge: Louisiana State University Press: 92. See also Norman R. Smith's 2010 *The Footprints of Black Louisiana*. Bloomington, IN: Xlibris: 107. For information on the location of the boys' home and the French Hospital, see Bowker Lee's census research.

- In her research, Bowker Lee looked at U.S. Census data from 1840 to 1930 to determine the demographics of the residents and business owners who occupied each block before the Lafitte Housing Development was built. Rachel Breunlin went through the individual blocks and noted patterns of ethnicity and jobs to create the "Mixing" section.

- For more on the pleasure gardens along the Carondelet Canal, see Luke Douglas' 2011 *Public Spaces, Private Gardens: A History of Designed Landscapes in New Orleans*. Baton Rouge: Louisiana State University Press: 76–82.

- Lafcadio Hearn's quote comes from *Inventing New Orleans: Writings of Lafcadio Hearn*, edited by S. Frederick Starr. Jackson: University Press of Mississippi: 38.

- History of Yvonne Busch and her students comes from Al Kennedy's 2005 *Chord Changes on the Chalkboard: How Public School Teachers Shaped Jazz and the Music of New Orleans*. Maryland: Scarecrow Press: 49–81. A recording of the Olympia Brass Band's version of "It Ain't My Fault" can be found on Mardi Gras Records' 2008 *The Ultimate Street Parade: New Orleans Brass Bands*.

- History on the Tremé Community Improvement Association comes from an interview with Ron Chisom by Rachel Breunlin in May of 2014. Leah Green's comments about residential councils come from Nelson 2005: 96. On reduction of federal funding to public housing, see the Council of Large Public Housing Authorities' "Public Housing and Housing Choice Voucher Funding History": http://www.clpha.org/uploads/Funding_Charts/1111 2013PHandHCVFundingHistory.pdf

- Hope Bland's reflections on living on Orleans Avenue come from Nelson 2005: 105.

- Ricky B's song "Shake Fo Yo Hood" can be found on Sinking City Records' 2013 release *B is for Bounce: New Orleans Rap Classics, 1994-1995*. Quotes from Ricky B come from Jules Bentley's 2013 article in *Antigravity*: http://www.antigravitymagazine.com/2013/04/signature-sound-hip-hop-legend-ricky-b-reflects-on-the-city-and-his-musical-legacy/

- Listen to the Soul Rebels' "Let Your Mind Be Free" at the beginning of this project's film, and also on Mardi Gras Record's 1995 title release.

- For more on the class action suit around lead poisoning in public housing, see http://www.law360.com/articles/252828/insurers-to-shell-out-65-5m-for-lead-paint-claims

REBUILDING AGAIN

- For a history of the activism around public housing in New Orleans, see Jay Arena's 2012 *Driven from New Orleans: How Nonprofits Betray Public Housing and Promote Privatization*. Minneapolis: University of Minnesota Press.

- For more information on secretary of HUD Alphonso Jackson's letter to Mayor C. Ray Nagin, see *The Times-Picayune*'s December 2007 article "HUD to Nagin: City Must Approve Demoliton of Lafitte": http://www.nola.com/news/index.ssf/2007/12/hud_to_nagin_city_must_approve.html

- For documentation on the expedited Section 106 review process for the Lafitte, see HANO's January 2007 "Section 106 Review and Documentation: Lafitte Housing Development, 15060165," compiled by U.S. Risk Management, L.L.C. For information about the community engagement process around the redevelopment of the Lafitte, see Providence Community Housing and Enterprise's 2007 "Homebuilding Plan for Tremé/Lafitte and Tulane/Gravier Community Development Approach."

• More on St. Ann's Parish can be found in David C. Estes' "The St. Ann Shrine in New Orleans: Popular Catholi   cism in Local, National, and International Contexts," available at: http://www.louisianafolklife.org/ LT/Articles_Essays/SaintAnnShrine.html. See also John Bernard Albert's 1998 dissertation, "Origins of Black Catholic Parishes in the Archdiocese of New Orleans, 1718–1920." Louisiana State University.

• More on the integration of the Bayou Road School can be found in Roger A. Fischer's 1974 *The Segregation Struggle in Louisiana: 1862–77*. Urbana: University of Illinois Press: 111–112. The Claiborne School is discussed in John W. Blassingame's 1973 *Black New Orleans: 1860–1880*. Chicago: University of Chicago Press: 120.

• For the 20th century history of the Bayou Road School and Joseph A. Craig, see Donald E. DeVore and Joseph Logsdon's 1991 *Crescent City Schools: Public Education in New Orleans 1841–1991*: Lafayette, LA: University of Louisiana at Lafayette Press: 199–204.

• Marcus Christian's research on civil rights activism in the 1920s is from in his chapter "Housing: 1900-1942" and "Stay In Your Own Backyard" in his unpublished manuscript *The History of Black Louisiana*, which is housed at the University of New Orleans' Louisiana Collection. For more on Christian himself, see Violet Harrington Bryan's chapter "Shaping Patterns of Myth and Folklore: The Federal Writer's Projects" in her 1993 book *The Myth of New Orleans in Literature: Dialogues of Race and Gender*. Knoxville: University of Tennessee Press: 95–114.

• For a fascinating history of Muslim Bengalis in New Orleans in the late 1800s, see Viveck Bald's 2015 reprint of *Bengali Harlem and the Lost Histories of South Asian America*. Boston: Harvard University Press: 54.

• For an overview of early history of public housing, see Alex F. Schwartz's 2010 *Federal Housing Policy*. New York: Routleldge. For more on federal housing policy and slum clearance in New Orleans, see Danny Ryan Gray's 2012 dissertation, "Effacing the 'Imagined Slum': Space, Subjectivity, and Sociality at the Margins of New Orleans." University of Chicago.

LAFITTE YEARS

• Research on the selection process of tenants for public housing can be found in Marnie Mahoney's 1985 M.A. thesis, "The   Changing Nature of Public Housing in New Orleans, 1930–1974." Tulane University: 31–32.

• A discussion of site selection for public housing around New Orleans can be found in HANO's *1937 Annual Report*, located in the New Orleans Public Library's City Archives.

• Leah Chase's reflections about black-run restaurants can be found in Ashley Nelson's 2005 *The Combination*. New Orleans: The Neighborhood Story Project/The Center for the Book at the University of New Orleans: 36–38.

• A discussion of urban renewal and the I-10 highway construction can be found in Michael Crutcher's 2010 *Tremé: Race and Place in a New Orleans Neighborhood*. Athens: University of Georgia Press: 37–59.

• Quote from Tom Dent comes from his Summer 1977 article "Designs for Claiborne Avenue" published in *Black River Journal: Notes from New Orleans*. Thanks to Jacques Morial and Helen Regis for sharing this issue with us.

• History of Clark Senior High comes from oral histories with Milton Batiste by Tad Jones and Barry Martyn that are housed in the Hogan Jazz Archive's oral history collection. For information about the history of Phillis Wheatley Elementary School, see the Historic American Buildings Survey No. LA-1453. For more details on the desegregation of public schools in New Orleans, see *Crescent City Schools*. History of the integration of John McDonogh Senior High comes from Rachel's research in John Mac yearbooks found at the Orleans Parish School Board Collection at the Louisiana Collection at the University of New Orleans.